Catfishing for Science: The Absurdity Behind Online Dating

Anonymous

Index

1- Introduction

In one of my previous books, *Yes, my Photos are Fake – and Why I do it: Catfishing in the First Person*, I argued that the practice nowadays called "catfishing" – the act of using others' photos in online services, such as social media or online dating – can actually be a good thing, since it allows people to see a part of other human beings which, in general, would be inaccessible to them. Across that same book, I also revealed some experiments that I once conducted with my best friend to attempt to verify the influence that photos of attractive people have in our online communication with others. Some of the results we obtained, back then, were immensely predictable – it will surprise absolutely nobody that people tend to prefer talking to an attractive person over an unattractive one – while others could be considered very unsettling, such as when we determined that if a man was attractive enough, even their most heinous acts would be explained away by those who are attracted to him, so they can continue to retain a positive image of the man they're talking to. As stated at the time, this would justify why, for example, people in an abusive relationship continue dating the abuser through all kinds of abuse, which, to an unbiased human being, would certainly seem like a very worrying issue. And yet, very few people seem to think about those problems, unless they, or a close friend of theirs, are actually in some sort of abusive relationship. At the same time, across the years I accidentally noticed that some parts of that broad panorama of online dating were changing. Nowadays, people aren't as tolerant, and dismissive of horrendous acts, as they were in the original experiment – in fact, in many cases people even seemed to have become a lot more intolerant than we'd expect – which is quite a positive change!

And then, one day, the whole Covid-19 pandemic started. All across the world people were asked not to leave their houses for a particular amount of time, for the sake of themselves and everyone else. As far as I could tell most did stay at home, and so did I. With nothing too significative to do, and out of pure boredom, I, like many other people, decided to create a whole new account in online dating apps and websites.

I picked three of the most popular ones and created the exact same account in each single one of them. The photos were the same, the text in each of the profiles equally so, and if anyone saw me in two different places, they would easily be able to recognise me. My point was not the one of misleading people at all, but just trying to talk to other human beings, and perhaps even meeting some new people. Nothing too fancy ever happened, I did manage to accomplish my basic goals, but across my personal usage of those three platforms I noticed that the world had changed. After the Covid-19 isolation periods ended I again found myself contemplating a wide variety of philosophical questions derived from my latest personal experience in those virtual environments. Some of them were fairly simple – How are the profiles we scroll through ordered? Why do we get many "likes" one day, and very few the next? ... – while others required extensive investigation. And that is what this new book is about, not only an attempt to recreate part of the experiments from before, but also trying to explore the limits and some lesser-known aspects of online dating.

Each chapter continues from the previous, almost as a story of my new personal journey through online dating, but it is also complemented with some almost-random curiosities derived from the topics being discussed.

===== Curiosities =====

1- Following the previous book, across the years I asked people from all over the world about the whole idea behind the "one lie". In a nutshell, "if you could, from the very beginning, avoid a broken heart by telling others a single lie, would you?" To this day, everyone always replied positively to that question, and as of the writing of these lines I was unable to find anyone who argues that one lie cannot be accepted if there are good reasons behind it.

2- Concerning my best friend, as referenced in the previous book she died a few years ago. No, I do not want to discuss that topic much further, but I want to dedicate this new book to her.

3- Why are people way less tolerant in online dating these days? This change fascinated me for months, until I came across a potential explanation – back in the day, profiles were presented to people one by one, and so there was a need to perform some tasks in order to advanced from the one you were seeing into the next one. At the time, this mechanic made it possible for users to individualize profiles and feel some kind of connection to the people behind them. However, nowadays the most famous online dating apps and websites work very differently, instead allowing their users to simply and quickly scroll across hundreds and hundreds of profiles without any real effort, which may be contributing to a dehumanization of each individual person, since you can just discard them away and pick a new one without any hassle.

4- But, when it comes to this change, how are other people's profiles ordered in their respective stacks? All online dating apps and websites tend to be very secretive about the specifics of their individual algorithms, but through extensive experimentation I was able to realize some broad aspects most of them seem to share:

- Profiles are rated based on who they "like" and who "likes" them. This numerical value, 0-10.00, is then used to determine other profiles presented to them, via a standard deviation from their current score. E.g. if you're internally rated a 5.00, you'll probably see people rated 3.00-7.00, which explains why we all see super attractive people at the very beginning, but start seeing less desirable ones later.
- Depending on who you "like", you may get more profiles similar to them. I noticed this when, by pure accident, I pressed the wrong option in a random profile from Kenya, as my very first "like", and then started being shown many other profiles from that same country.

5- Regarding the varying number of "likes" we may get from day to day, obviously those depend on other humans reacting positively to your profile, but depending on several aspects your profile may be displayed to more or less people. For example, many apps and websites of this nature instantly show your profile to a very significative number of people when you first register, in order to calculate your base score quickly (see above), but also to give you the idea that your new account is desirable and attempting to hook you up to that "new like" notification.

==========

2- My first profile... and what happened to it!

At first, I simply wanted to get to know other human beings. I was neither interested in meeting new casual sex partners, nor did I expect to get into any kind of romantic relationship. As such, if I was going to compile a personal profile once again, I promptly decided that I wanted to make it as realistic as possible, neither presenting myself as some sort of living god, nor doing just the bare minimum and hoping some people would like it. So, when creating my profile in three different apps and websites, I included my first name, my birth date, and a location 10 Km away from my own. When prompted for photos, the systems usually told me I had to include at least one or two, while others advised me to put up to six in there, but none of them allowed more than 10 photos per profile.

And so, what photos did I pick? Based on the content of the previous book, you'd possibly think I would be using false photos right away, but instead I decided to give these places an entirely new chance, something which required me to submit real photos of myself. For my very first one, I decided to go for a bit of a funny one – a photo with a stuffed Bulbasaur sitting over my head, taken at the Museum of Greek Mythology (in South Korea), which I hoped would capture both my love of Pokémon and some of my cultural travels.

For the second, I decided to joke around a bit with the subject of mirror selfies – I went to my room, took a photo where my face would be completely obscured by the camera flash, and then added a comic balloon to it, stating "Hey, please read my profile!" – by this sequence of actions, I was hoping to have a little fun and make potential readers realize that we're all human beings, not just photos in a screen.

For the third one, I presented a photo I was taken in front of some natural caves in my country – an allusion to my interest in visiting unusual places, specially since the caves I had visited are mostly unknown to people outside of their respective area.

Three other photos were also selected at the

same time, but they were only added to the profiles later – a photo of myself along with some stuffed animals, greek vases, medieval manuscripts and old paintings, which I hoped would display my many cultural interests in a single image; a photo where I was impeccably well dressed, taken during a post-Covid business lunch, so people could see how I look in a suit (in spite of the fact I was wearing a protective mask); and a photo taken by my best friend during our last travel, where you could see me walking in a famous Spanish city, as another indicative of my many travels.

Then, I also had to fill the text which would be presented in my profile. For the sake of the whole experience, I decided to fill literally all of the basic fields each application and website offered. So, when it came down to talking about myself, all the profiles I created had this information, either in this original form or simplified a bit (by editing the first paragraph and simplifying the second):

"*What I lack in fanciful photos of myself, I compensate for with amazing dialogues, potential visits to awesome places, and the ability to make people laugh even when they're feeling down.*

About me? In a nutshell – Award-winning Author. Bulbasaur Picker. Cultured. Dislikes Social Media. Ex-Traveller. Funny. Great with Kids. Has an Auto-immune Disease. Knowledge-seeker. Lover of the Arts, Dialogues, Literature and Nature. Night Owl. Philanthropist. Researcher. Sweet and Friendly. Talkative. Unusual. Volunteer with orphans and animals.

If you identify with any of this, or you simply want to talk for a while, feel free to drop me a message!"

But one of the websites I ended up trying to use allowed me to include further information about myself. In that sequence, and when prompted for my current goals, I mentioned: "*I'd love to survive the pandemic, collaborate with even more companies around the globe, increase my donations to charities, and perhaps even finally write a PhD thesis on a more valuable subject*".

Regarding a potential worst quality, I stated that mine was *"Actually caring about other human beings. I always wish I could give people a huge hug and some words of sympathy when they're down, regardless of who they are and where they live"*.

Concerning what I really love about myself, *"I know my limits, my strengths and my weaknesses. I'm not here to pretend to be the greatest man alive, nor do I intentionally try to sound much better than I really am (although I may sound a bit unfunny in these lines)."*

Being asked about six things I could never do without, I followed through by pointing out that *"I live a simple life, and I enjoy it like that. Therefore, my daily needs are very basic – literature, food, water, dialogues, and medicine. And yes, I am aware that's only five, but caution requires me to save the sixth for later. Or you can take it and use the remaining one yourself, if you prefer...?"*

I also mentioned my favourite conspiracy theory, *"There is a conspiracy theory that says that all conspiracy theories are actually true, but they are spread by governments in very silly ways in order to pre-emptively discredit people who may try to leak inconvenient facts. Is this true? I'm not really sure, but it is funny and it does make some sense!"*

When prompted for my definition of a perfect day, I said that *"I do not believe a 'perfect day' can be planned in advance. For me, it can only be built in that unexpected stage we tend to call life, perhaps with an amazing person by my side; it is the charming 4-way mixture of the unexpected, the desired, the company and the connection which can, in my personal opinion, turn any day into a perfect one!"*

Then being asked to admit a private thing, I did so with the following information: *"Due to my auto-immune disease and the Covid pandemic I currently have to spend most of my time at home. That's one of the main reasons why I created this profile – although I have zero interest in casual stuff, I do love talking to people!"*

And, to finalize, what was I really seeking? *"An*

interesting person who wants to have amazing
dialogues, visit almost-forgotten places, and help us
both learn all kinds of new and interesting things. Is
that you? If so, do send me a message!"

Apart from all of this information, I naturally
also filled all the other sections the same website
requested of me, such as my height, ethnicity, the
languages I speak, information on potential college
degrees, my job and religion, among others, to ensure
that this profile not only was completely filled, but also
fairly represented the person I really am. Besides, in
order to ensure such accuracy, I also asked some of
my friends to read it, and they all agreed that I really
was the person portrayed all across the photos and
through the text. This made me feel confident that
maybe the world had changed significantly, that
maybe people didn't care just about photos any more,
which would be a great thing.

Having created the profile described above,
which took me a few hours, I then decided to see what
other profiles were available. For each one that I
passed my eyes across, I tried to focus exclusively on

16

what the profile said, as I considered all the photos holly secondary. Here and there, I spotted some people I would genuinely like to get to know better, and so I "liked" their profile, and further sent them an initial message, when available, explaining why I wanted to get to know them and what attracted me to their profile. Meanwhile, I also tried to keep track of the number of people who supposedly wanted to talk to me, although I made no special effort to chase any of those. I felt the process was going great, and I was honestly hoping that some of the people I was interested in getting to know better would contact me back.

Then, an entire week passed but none of those people ever wrote me back, which really disappointed me. At the same time, about 30 people had liked my profile, but even when such an option available, none of them ever bothered sending me any kind of initial text. Maybe my photos were no good? Maybe nobody liked what I had written in the profiles? Maybe... a thousand different possibilities soon rose in my head, the most significant of which was that maybe people were even more addicted to photos nowadays. In spite of the fact I had gone through all the trouble of making the best profile I could, one which undoubtedly captured who I really was as a person, very few people seemed to be interested in any of it. And so, I quickly realized that if I was going to try online dating, I had to take a very different approach.

===== Curiosities =====

1- "Bare minimum" and "low-effort" seem to be two significant keywords in online dating, since most people appear not to significantly fill their profiles at all. Instead, they just create that space, add some photos to it, and hope to get their "likes" and messages. Personally, I always found the idea absurd, instead preferring to talk about myself in the profiles as much as possible, as I hope that will garner the interest of others who share interests similar to mine.

2- As you may recall, I included in my profile "a location 10 Km away from my own". This was fully intended – if, for an online dating profile, you are allowed to input your current location, the company you work for, or even the place you study in, it is generally a good idea to either omit those, or present some information which is not completely true. You never know who is going to read your profile, what their intentions towards you are, and so it is important to protect yourself from potentially crazy people!

3- If you look it up online, there are some basic guidelines regarding what kind of photos people should submit to online dating in order to generate maximum interest in them. I was perfectly aware of those guidelines, but instead decided to include in my profile quaint photos which represented who I really am, instead of, let's say, including a photo taken next to a private swimming pool, or next to an expensive car, just to make myself seem more impressive.

4- Although I chose to completely fill my profile with all the requested information, not everyone does this. If you decide to go for a profile that focuses highly on photos – like many people do – you may want to provide as little information as possible, since any kind of data provided by you may contribute to make others like your profile less. A common strategy appears to be crowding a profile with beautiful photos and then letting others imagine whatever they want from them.

5- Remember when I mentioned that "about 30 people had liked my profile"? An interesting thing I determined through my experiments in online dating apps is that some of those "likes" were not really from other human beings, but issued through bots created by the companies themselves, in order to artificially inflate the number of likes you get. This tends to happen frequently in services where you cannot see who liked you without paying some money, and so, by inflating those numbers – which usually happens in a sudden jump on the very first day, or in small trickles through time – people are more likely to subscribe to the premium version of their services. DON'T DO IT, EVER, this is just a trick from them, and it is not worth it at all, because even if you match those people, they're fake profiles. It should even be noted there were already some court cases about this practice in the past, and so it is widely known that some very big companies do this, such as the owner of *Match.com* !

6- Although this book focuses on male profiles and their personal online dating experience, at one point I was suggested that I should attempt a similar experiment with a female profile too. I did so in the past but did not retry it here, for the simple reason that, based on data collected at the time (and which was briefly discussed in *Yes, my Photos are Fake – and Why I do it: Catfishing in the First Person*), even with an absolute minimum-effort profile, one with a single photo and zero textual content, such a person would still get a significant number of "likes" and introductory messages. And, in fact, some of the data collected for this book even points in that direction, since it shows that a significant number of women have very low-content profiles and yet men go to talk to them[1].

========

---

1   For more information, check "Annex 1".

3- My second profile

My realistic profile was going nowhere very, very quickly. The people I wanted to talk to, if they really saw my profile, did not appear to be interested in how I portrayed myself, either because of my photos or due to how I portrayed myself in the textual sections. And while, originally, I was hoping that such realistic portrayal of myself, in all that it mean to be me, would be enough to attract the kind of people I would enjoy talking to, the whole idea was simply failing. I felt I needed to know why, and for that reason I decided to repeat part of the experiment I had performed with my best friend back in the day.

I deleted my first profile, the one described in the previous chapter, and instead decided to open a different one in the exact same places. However, I also felt that to create another one just for the sake of it would be a huge waste of time. Instead, if I was going to do this all over again, I felt I had to collect as much data as possible, in order to present to people what online dating is really all about. For that reason, I documented each single step of the process, and we'll now be going through all of it.

Based on the experiments from a few years ago, the ones described in the previous book, from the get-go I assumed that the reason why my profile was just not getting that many matches was the photos, and the photos alone. In order to test that possibility, I had to create a new profile where I retained all the essential basics from the previous one, but changed all the photos and reworded the main text. This way, the significant kernel of who makes me who I am would still be there, and I would know that a significant change in the number of "likes" would be all about the photos.

In order to grab new photos for this experiment, I simply created an empty *Instagram* profile – I really do not use that app – and decided to check popular tags related to men. For hours, I looked through near-endless photos presented in hashtags such as #hotmen and #doglover, until I realized this could pose some serious ethical concerns. So, I instead contacted a few photographers in the same app and explained them what I wanted to do. One of them, a photographer from Germany which preferred to remain anonymous, found the whole idea very interesting, and so he put me in touch with one of his new models, who was kind enough to allow me to use any of his personal photos under a small rule – I had to edit and change them a bit, so they wouldn't be easily traced back to his real identity. I was more than happy to accept that condition, and so I continued to be myself but through the photos became this "John".

For the new profile's first photo, I picked one of John's photos where he was holding a really cute puppy, and edited the background to display a beautiful pink flower field near Mount Fuji, in Japan. Based on this reconstruction, the profile would supposedly show "me" with one of the puppies I volunteer with, but also present potential readers with one of my many travels.

The second photo was one at the beach, which I edited to show a beach very different from the original one. Since this photo heavily displayed John's prominent muscles, I assumed it would be very popular with the ladies.

The third photo was also at the beach, with John now fully dressed and looking away from the camera; again, I edited it to display the exact same beach shown in the previous photo, but from a different angle, as if they had both been taken in the same day.

The fourth one showed John's beautiful smile, which I edited to be presented at the top of a local mountain, while the fifth, originally of John's beautiful eyes looking at the camera, was edited to make their colour even more prominent.

The sixth, and final one, was a photo of John modelling, with a big hat and glasses – I changed the background to move the whole scene to the local forest. So, in a nutshell, I grabbed six of John's photos, and, with his permission, changed them in order to make them more alike of environments in my area and things I myself tend to do.

Next, I had to fill the profile once again. Based on the content from my initial one, but also to test if the whole problem was only about the images being presented, I grabbed my initial text and changed it to maintain the original meaning but sound just a bit different. And so, in case you have forgotten by now, my original presentation text said:

"*What I lack in fanciful photos of myself, I compensate for with amazing dialogues, potential visits to awesome places, and the ability to make people laugh even when they're feeling down.*

About me? In a nutshell – Award-winning Author. Bulbasaur Picker. Cultured. Dislikes Social Media. Ex-Traveller. Funny. Great with Kids. Has an Auto-immune Disease. Knowledge-seeker. Lover of the Arts, Dialogues, Literature and Nature. Night Owl. Philanthropist. Researcher. Sweet and Friendly. Talkative. Unusual. Volunteer with orphans and animals.

If you identify with any of this, or you simply want to talk for a while, feel free to drop me a message!"

This text, when simplified (particularly due to

the character limit of some apps), would retain just the second paragraph. I got that one, quickly cooked up a new first phrase, and came up with this alternative version:

"I'm not much into online stuff, but friends told me to give this place a try.

I'm a book author, cultured, former world traveller, volunteer with animals and orphans, nature hiker, I also love arts and literature, a bit of a night owl, a PhD researcher, but here... in this place, I'm just a man looking for a woman who is actually worth getting to know better."

Unlike before, I did not fill any other profile sections, leaving it all to people's imagination, and so I soon started using this new profile as my own.

===== Curiosities =====

1- Most online dating apps and websites track

your data even after you have deleted your profile[2]. Some seem to do it for a number of days presented in their "Privacy Policy", while others may retain partial data forever, under very vague "security reasons" and "profile identification processes". As such, if you ever want to really try an experiment like this one, or simply get a completely fresh start with your profile, you have to start by completely deleting your current one and then obtain some or all of the following, depending on the data you've provided it before:

- A new IP address;
- A new phone number and e-mail address;
- An entirely new Facebook account;
- New photos (see section "3" below);
- A new phone and/or desktop;
- New accounts in social media that you may want to link to your new online dating account.

Of course some of these are easier to get than others, but there are a few workarounds to avoid having to purchase a new phone and/or desktop, such as simply changing the device ID. Overall, and in a nutshell, in order to get a truly fresh start in any of those places

---

2   For an example of the data collected by a specific app check "Annex 8".

(otherwise, you'll be penalized in ways which include, but are not limited to, decreased visibility by other members and higher prices for everything), you always need to ensure that absolutely no data is retained in common between profiles, or their services will be able to identify you and give you a non-fresh experience.

2- Nowadays, some online dating apps and websites require – or allow – you to verify your profile by taking a very specific photo or video. Nobody ever seems to read privacy policies, but this is essentially a sort of scam on their side, since they want to obtain your facial geometry, which they do not always delete after said verification (and may even end up selling in the future). This way, if you ever created a new profile in the future and used other photos of yourself, they would still be able to identify you without much effort. For these reasons, I strongly suggest you never verify your profile, even more since doing so is not an indicative of the person being credible – if nothing else, you can even easily verify your own fake profile by taking advantage of so-called "Deepfake" systems and apps, which allow you to look any way you want in your photos or videos.

3- However, online dating apps and websites may also retain *other* personal information about your account(s) that may help identify you, which include, but are not limited to:

- You name(s);
- Your birth date;
- Any kind of textual information you wrote in your profile;
- Your reported location, and often the GPS coordinates where you created your profile;
- Past messages you've sent to other people;
- Any of the photos you may have used before, even if you change them in some basic ways;
- Information on any potential purchases;
- All the activities you performed while logged in.

4- Still regarding "Privacy Policies" and "Terms of Service", almost nobody ever seems to bother reading through those, but they frequently feature very interesting pieces of information. For example, did you know that by signing for a certain very famous app and website, you actually give their entire content network permission to use your photos and personal information in any way they like, including creating fake profiles of their own? To a general reader, this could seem like a very big deal, and yet most people pay no attention to what they're accepting when they sign up for an account, and seem to be absolutely clueless about this.

5- Depending on your jurisdiction, using other people's photos as your own may be illegal. For that reason, if you want to try an experiment like the one I disclose here, please make sure there are no laws against it in your area!

6- You could be wondering why I picked those six specific photos from John, or why I edited them in the way I did. Overall, I had some limited material to work with – a grand total of 65 photos, some of them very similar in content – and out of those original photos I had to pick those which seemed to match the basic guidelines for the photos most liked in online dating, as alluded to at the end of the previous chapter. And then, I simply had some vague inspiration to edit them in the way I did, trying not to make them seem either completely fake or too beautiful. The ways in which they were edited were not planned in advance at all, they simply came to me while I was looking at the original photos.

7- How could I make sure that John's photos weren't traceable to their original source? There are many websites which allow you to do such a verification, but the most popular (and free) ones appear to be *Google Images* and *Tineye*. Simply upload one of your photos to both of those and see if it gets any matches to their original content – in case it does, that means you still need to change your photo even more, so it won't be so easily recognised by the automated algorithms and personal verification that most apps and websites now use.

==========

32

4- One person, two faces

So, simplistically, I had created a profile which I felt represented me fairly well, and nobody seemed very interested in talking to it, even when I was able to approach them with an initial message. Then, I created a second one, which still represented who I really am as a person, but instead featured someone else's photos. And following through with the new idea, I also decided that I would not be the one to message anyone at all first, even when such option was directly provided to me – otherwise, the fact they were contacting me could be attributed by some to the message itself, instead of exclusively to the actual content of the profile.

The numbers of people who "liked" this second profile raised significantly and steadily from those first few minutes on, to the point I even reached the number of 30 in way less than an hour (an achievement which, as you may recall, took an entire week for the other profile). Without much effort, this seemed to prove that people were liking the new profile just because of its pretty photos, as I had feared, but things soon became even worse, when other users even started sending me their own initial messages.

The very first message I got was from a 28 year old woman from Campo Grande, Brazil[3]. She sent me a fairly long message, where she presented herself to me and concluded with the words *"Just message back if you think we could match"*. She seemed deeply religious, eager for marriage, to find what she herself called *"the dad of my children"*, and I quickly noticed a problem – this felt as if she hadn't read my profile at all, as if she was simply sending me the exact same message she had previously sent to many other men, as if we were all some kind of fish and she was trying to capture just any one of us. If I wasn't conducting an experiment, would I have messaged her back? I'm absolutely sure I wouldn't, because I couldn't see anything in her profile, or even in her (optional) initial message, that made me feel we could connect in a significant way.

---

3   Some of the biographical information presented here and elsewhere was slightly changed for privacy reasons.

But, even if this first profile who contacted me was just a complete fluke for me, now people were indeed contacting me, even when they knew close to nothing about who I really was, unlike before, unlike when I extensively provided them with a very significative and real depiction of myself. But, in a positive sense, this allowed me to synthesize a simple version of the interest I had in other's profiles – there were some photos, usually ranging between 1 and 10; some profile text, which may range from literally 0 characters up to veritable epic poems; and a potential initial message, where someone is allowed to send you just one piece of text, supposedly to entice you into writing back to them.

Unfortunately, no current apps or websites appear to feature a way of checking how many people truly saw your profile, but over the period of a week this second profile was "liked" by 2343 people. Out of those, 184 were even so interested in it that they decided to send it an initial message. And this would all be perfectly acceptable, until we realize that the first profile only got 30 "likes" over the same period, and nobody even bothered writing any initial messages to it. To me, this represented an absurdly high increment in "likes" exclusively based on photos and nothing else, and so I felt that I needed to research further into who was actually acting positively towards this profile

===== Curiosities =====

1- Generally, in these apps and websites you can only check who "liked" your profile through paid options. However, since I naturally didn't want to get any of the premium options for the services at hand, I cheated a bit and used alternative ways to gather that information, which, based on their illegality, I cannot fully disclose. However, if you are truly curious about how to do this, you may be able to find some online resources which present bugs and technical flaws in your favourite online dating apps and websites.

2- In both profiles, shortly after their creation something very curious happened in a particular online dating website – I did not have any kind of "likes" for a bit, but after a few short minutes the numbers unexpectedly jumped to 14. When I checked the identity of those people, I realized they were all from third-world countries and, in a very odd way, precisely the same ones for both profiles. Meaning, if you created a profile in this one place, early on you'll always get a small boost of likes, possibly as a way to seduce you into buying their premium subscription, and if you actually do that, you'll quickly find yourself in the middle of a potentially undesirable group of people who appear to like all profiles, supposedly because they're not even human at all, but bots designed by the same creators of the website.

3- When it comes down to sending people an initial message – an option that only a limited number of websites and apps have available – I always felt it is best to reference something you can see in the current profile, in order to assure to your potential reader that you have actually paid attention to who they are.

4- Why is it that most dating apps and websites do not allow you to see the number of people who simply passed across your profile, while generally allowing you to see those who liked it? I always assumed this absence has to do with the fact that providing such a data could prove very frustrating to their users, e.g. "2000 people came here but only 1 liked me?!", which could lead them to stop using the service.

==========

5- Who contacted this profile?

Out of all the people who "liked" the second profile and also messaged it, I jotted down some brief notes about each one of them, such as – their age; their self-reported location; the content of their initial message; their number of photos; the general content of their profile; and whether I would usually message them back, based on all the elements they provided[4]. Such information makes it possible to trace a broad overview of all the people who decided to message it.

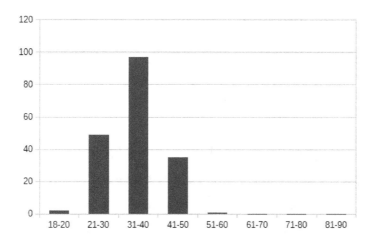

---

4   For the complete data collected here, check "Annex 1".

First, when it comes to their age, the youngest person was just 18 years old, while the oldest was 52, but the most common cluster was clearly below 40 years of age[5]. This makes sense because, for anthropological reasons, most women tend to prefer older men, and since my profile stated I was 37 years old, the data collection confirms what would be expected, although there were also some slightly older people, in a smaller number, who also sent me their messages.

Philippines	38 (+ 46)
Indonesia	43
US	14
Thailand	12
Brazil	10
Kenya	9
Other countries (total)	58

Regarding their self-reported location[6], although people from 44 different countries seem to have contacted me, their most common location was the Philippines and Indonesia, with almost half the

---

5   For more information, check "Annex 2".
6   For complete information on all the countries check "Annex 3".

messages. And this definitely begs the question, why were so many people from those two countries messaging me, and yet, more often than not, doing so in a very low-effort way? I believe that two main reasons may have contributed for this.

First, in western culture women are accustomed to men always giving the first step, and so, although a high number of people from many western countries "liked" my profile, those women generally tend to hope that men like them too and then end up contacting them first. In order to test this possibility, I started by moving my profile to New York, US, where I quickly got a very high number of "likes", but only two initial messages. Then, I installed a dating app in which, upon sharing a mutual "like", local women are always required to message men first, and with very few exceptions the initial messages they sent me were either low-effort (more often than not, something as quick and simple as a mere "Hello"), or they would find some way around it, typically by sending me some kind of animated GIF – and then, if I didn't start undeniably taking the lead (e.g. if I just sent them a "hello" in return, or replied with a GIF of my own), the conversation would never go anywhere at all.

A second explanation may lie on the fact that women from these two countries tend to see foreigners, specially ones from Europe and North America, as a good way towards a better life, and so, by sending them many low-effort messages – which are quicker than making custom-made ones for everyone they approach – they hope that someone may bite their bait and talk to them, potentially leading to some kind of relationship which may end up profiting them. I can openly acknowledge that this view of the world may seem racist to a completely unbiased reader, and so I felt that this possibility needed further testing, in order to confirm or refute its veracity. In order to do so, I created a new profile in the same app, gave it the basic name "John" (which also appears to be very common in that country), placed it in the Manila, added only photos with dark glasses (so my eyes couldn't be seen, which could betray my real origins), and claimed in the profile I was from the Phillipines. This lead to almost no likes, but when, after approximately 48 hours, I emended the profile to replace just a single word, simply changing that country's name to "Germany", I suddenly started getting way more likes. And so, whether you want to call this theory racist or not, the data appears to confirm it.

But what about the other four main countries I received messages from? A significant number of contacts from the US makes perfect sense, since the main audience for the dating apps and websites I was using is that country. Thailand may fall under the same reasons as the two countries discussed above, but I can openly admit I did not test if the same issues discussed above also occurred here. For Brazil, since my profile claimed I was in Portugal and spoke Portuguese, getting a significant number of messages from people in that country is fairly common. And, regarding Kenya, I was unsure on what could be going on until I directly connected with someone from that country[7]. She wanted to have an "interracial relationship" with someone, but also had a huge interest in involving herself, romantically and sexually, with a "Caucasian" – for that reason, chances are that

---

7   See "Message Proposal 27" in "Annex 1", or read across the next chapter for more information on why this contact happened and what ultimately happened with it.

44

at least some other people from that country were also contacting me over the simple fact my skin was white. And, in fact, other users from the same country also contacted me, with a message sent to another test profile even saying "Would you be interested in black women?", which further supports this idea[8].

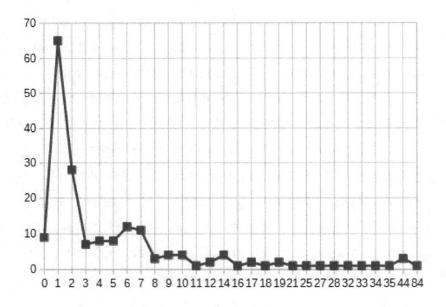

But, in those rare cases in which people did send me an initial message (when such a possibility was available), how many words did they write to

<hr />

8   Regarding the usage of this secondary test profile, some notes are made later.

me[9]? Of course there are some notable exceptions –
for example, three different people sent me a total of
44 words, and one even produced a message with 84!
– but the vast majority of people sent me just a single
word, usually a "Hello" or some equivalent to it.
Although in a more real environment this may seem
strange, it also confirms an idea already presented
before, that when most women are put in the spotlight
and asked to write an initial message on their own,
they go for the bare minimum and hope that, picking
up from their clue, a man then follows and does all the
work for them.

---

9   For more information, check "Annex 4".

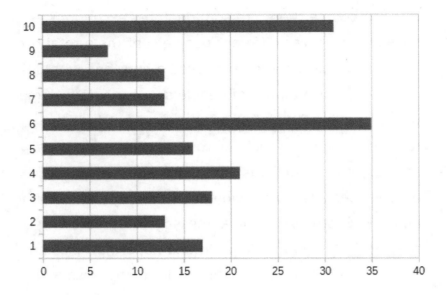

And why would they do so? As determined in the previous book, most women – and men too, I would certainly argue – seem to go for looks, first and foremost. And, in the same way they'd like to find an attractive man, they tend to present multiple photos of themselves in their profile – as investigated here[10], the highest numbers of women appear to have either 10 photos in their profile (the absolute highest number permitted in the apps and websites I used), or simply 6 (the maximum number in some apps, but which others also suggest as the optimal one). Given the fact

---

10 For more information, check "Annex 5".

that many of those profiles feature little textual information, this data makes it sound that women are going for looks but also trying to provide such looks themselves, seemingly without considering they are actually human beings and that there is more to life that looks alone.

Another important element, out of almost 200 people who wrote me a message over this period of a week, I felt I would usually – i.e. outside of this experiment – write back to only about 11 of them, which represents a rate of about 6% of the people who wrote to me. At this point, there is always someone who chooses to see only the positive side of the whole situation, i.e. "sure, you went through all that trouble, you lost a ton of your time, but at the very least you found 11 people to talk to!!!", but how real is that idea? Were those eleven people actually worth all the trouble? And, perhaps even more important for a general reader, would any of them turn into *love*?

===== Curiosities =====

1- For this whole experiment, it proved to be very difficult to synthesize the actual content of people's profiles. However, there is a trend that certainly deserves to be noted here – a significant number of profiles contain a simple phrase alike of "Ask me", indicating that it features little textual information but a potential reader is free to ask them (anything?) they want. I always felt this is the most noteworthy indicative of a low-effort profile, and usually it is even a good indicative that the person behind it is not actually worth talking to.

2- Why I didn't get any messages from people over 52 years of age is easy to explain – they rarely use apps. In fact, out of all the years I've used online dating, both personally and as part of experiments, I can only remember having talked to one person above that age, a woman of over 60 years old who lived nearby and was looking for new friends, but also very rarely logged in to the app.

3- For more information on how foreign men are treated in the Philippines, you can watch TV shows such as the "90 Days" series – in that one, whenever a woman is from that country, it is frequently discussed if she was also texting many other men "from America", something they always deny, until being shown clear evidence of the opposite.

4- For women, a similar high number of messages from men in India may occur, where sometimes they even request the sending of photos of what is now satirized as "bobs and vagana". Investigating this other topic, I eventually found out this may happen because in the culture of India, and even in some Bollywood movies, white women are represented as very open and sexually libertine (unlike native ones, they believe). So, it seems that some local men are led to suppose they are very open to sexual topics.

5- Going back a bit, for the test profile for the Philippines I picked the name "John" after investigating the most common male names in that country. Essentially, I wanted to select one which was common in western culture but also in that country's own culture.

6- The fact so many people were sending me just *one word* in their initial messages is baffling. Can you imagine going to a bar, talking to a random person and trying to make them interested in you by uttering a single initial word, as opposed to a complete phrase? Unless you're extremely attractive, chances are that it wouldn't work at all, and yet people mysteriously seem to think that such a strategy would work in an online environment – and if it ever does, it is possibly because many men may be so desperate that any women at all may, to them, seem better than none.

7- Although I noted down the number of photos in each profile, I'm sure that evaluating the actual content of those images would be a much more interesting thing. However, given the fact that performing such a task would lead to many disputable assertions, I could not find any good way to do it, except for the negative cases in which those pictures are heavily edited, feature memes, or just contain quotes.

===========

6- Talking to people

As already stated at the end of the previous chapter, out of all the people who wrote a message to the second profile I eventually found 11 that I would talk to under normal conditions. Out of those, I randomly selected five of them, to ensure I was not biased in my choices, and attempted to talk to each one as I would normally do.

The first one was "message proposal 7"[11], a 45 year old woman living in Thailand who claimed not to be "into the online stuff either (...) [but instead] looking for someone who is worth traveling for, and maybe even relocating for". As I would typically do, I started by asking her how her day was going, to which she replied that she had been talking to her brother, and quickly asked me if I had any siblings myself. I found the sequence of events a bit strange – usually, people tend to ask me about my own day, instead of instantly changing the topic to something else – but

---

11 For this and all the other message proposals mentioned here, check "Annex 1".

told her I did have a brother. After I told her this, I did not receive any more answers from her for the rest of the week, even though I clearly saw her logging in, and later logging out, of her profile a few times.

Next, I talked to the person from "message proposal 27", a 26 year old woman from Kenya who had a very complete profile. Ours was a very strange conversation, with she openly admitting, from the very beginning, that she was seeking an "interracial relationship" and had sent me a message because she wanted to involve herself, romantically and sexually, with a "Caucasian". The conversation followed through with her asking me many strange questions, such as whether I'd consider a long-term and long-distance relationship, or when would I be able to visit her in Kenya myself, before settling for purely sexual topics – and all of this just in a first conversation! Apart from a bit offensive and too hasty, I also found her dialogue with me profoundly racist, as she reduced me exclusively to the colour of my skin, and I ended up completely closing down the conversation with her after just a few minutes.

The third person I talked to was the one from "message proposal 139", a 48 year old woman from New York who appeared to consider me "so sweet and amazing". These words made me particularly curious on how she even knew that about me, but it seems that hers were just completely blank compliments – in fact, she hadn't even really given much thought to my profile, and when approached on her initial words, she quickly changed the subject and instead asked me, as one of her very first questions, "What do you do? What are you researching?" When I answered her two questions, and in spite of the fact she had essentially ignored my own, I was left unanswered for the rest of the week.

Next one was the person from "message proposal 145", a 36 year old woman from Guatemala who had a photo of herself seemingly receiving a goalkeeping award. In her initial message, she had described herself as "glad" over the fact I had created my profile. I messaged her about it, she asked me how my day was going, I answered her, but after almost a week had elapsed she hadn't answered me back yet. When I finally decided to ask about her silence, she suddenly told me "I don't see the app that much lol", which she quickly followed with a "sorry" and a "How are you?", which was exactly the same question she had already asked me a few days before, and which, when I answered it, she simply ignored. I decided to answer it once again, and again I was left without any kind of reply for the rest of the week.

The last person I approached was the one from "message proposal 153", a 37 year old single parent from North Carolina, US, who, in her initial message, had told me she was "teach[ing] and working on my PhD in science education". All seemed to be going well, and we had a good dialogue in that very first day, following which she told me she had to take her young kid to school. I never heard back from her again, even though I repeatedly saw her profile logging in and out, until the moment I closed down the second profile.

And so, out of the five people I had randomly chosen to talk to, none of them ever went anywhere significative. But maybe I was simply unlucky in those random choices, maybe a different combination of five other people would lead to different results, and that made me realize there was still a final test that I needed to try with this second profile.

===== Curiosities =====

1- Perhaps I could have try to talk to all 11 people, but not only would that be more time-consuming, but I also wanted to create a more realistic environment, in which a man doesn't always answer to all people who message him. Plus, even if I had answered back to all of them, the case could always be made that one of the many people I had not talked to would have acted very differently... which, ultimately, would have required me to talk to pretty much everyone, even people with extremely low-effort profiles, that I would never approach in a real environment.

2- Maybe this is part of my local culture, but I have the habit of staring conversations – after the initial message, that is – by asking people how their day is going. This, because if someone is having a really crappy day, maybe they will act very differently towards you than they usually would, and so you could end up accidentally losing a great opportunity to meet someone new.

3- Regarding sexual topics in conversations, I always felt those are perfectly okay if both people involved are fine with it. However, in the one case discussed in this chapter, I felt it was extremely weird that the other person went for sexual topics right away, and ended up blocking her profile over it.

4- One of the women I talked to told me she doesn't check the app very much. This raises many significative questions (e.g. how does she even expect to meet anyone, acting like that?), but more often than not such words tend to be used simply as a scam, as a way to redirect the person to some other app or means of contact. Nowadays, phrases such as "I don't talk much here, but if you gave me your *Instagram* we'd be able to talk a lot more in there" are fairly common, mostly as a trick to check your other social media.

==========

7- Talking to people (again)

As a final test for the second profile I decided that I had to try to talk to completely random people. So, in each app and website I was using at that time, I simply read the first five profiles I came across, "liked" them and, where available, sent them an initial message somehow related to their profile, as I would have done in my first of these two profiles. In less than 24 hours, at least three of those five profiles had connected with my own in each app or website. None of them seemed particularly noteworthy to me – remember, they had been picked completely at random, without any intellectual reasons for those choices – but there was one specific woman I remember for very sad reasons.

She was 27 years old and based in Florida, US. We talked perfectly for two or three days, because she was going through some really rough times in her life and I was genuinely trying to help her. Then, at one point, she asked me for my *Instagram* username, and I explained her that I didn't have one, since I truly feel that app/website promotes too high of an emphasis on photos alone. Instead, I tried to give her my own *Whatsapp* number, but for some unexplained reason she was unable to add it. She then kept on badgering me about photos, more and more, and eventually blocked my profile, possibly over the fact I hadn't catered to her repeated demands.

Her actions truly saddened me, because there I was, honestly trying to help this young-ish woman over what seemed to be a really tough period of her life, and all that mattered to her were... more photos (!), and only those, as if my entire existence could be resumed into just a small number of static snapshots. And yet, her case was not an entirely unique one. Across the years, and through my personal and professional experience in the areas of online dating, I've seen people developing a completely obsessive relationship with *Instagram*, to the point those who do not use it are too often and almost instantly labelled as "fake". And so, I finally realized, once and for all, that online dating was all about the fantasy of photos, and little about who people really are, deep inside.

===== Curiosities =====

1- In the context at hand, people tend to use many different ways to redirect you to their *Instagram*. "I don't use this app much, but if you added my *Instagram* we could talk more..." was already mentioned in the previous chapter, but other popular techniques are:

- Claiming they are going to delete their current profile but want to keep in touch with you;
- Presenting people with just one photo, a very attractive one, and then claiming they have more on their other social media... where, very conveniently, their profile is private and can't be seen without adding it;
- Supposedly wanting to ensure that you are really you;
- Wanting "proof of life", i.e. if you claim to do so-and-so, you must have photos of it in your profile, right?!

2- This constant reliance on *Instagram* for a supposed identity verification begs a massive question

– if someone ever wanted to trick them, why not create a fake profile in that other app, fill it with fake photos, purchase some followers (2.30€ for 100 followers, last time I checked), purchase some "likes" (1.50€ for 100 of those, last time I checked), and pretend to be real? I asked this same question to many people and, ultimately, nobody was able to give me a good answer to it. So, all things considered, an *Instagram* account can be faked, and if you want to give an extra layer of appearing to be real to your fake profile, you can easily do it by adding some photos to it and purchasing a few euros or dollars worth of followers and "likes".

3- Chances are that people aren't even asking for others' usernames to do profile verifications, but simply to get more followers in their accounts, as supported by the fact that many of the profiles I read literally contained the person's *Instagram* username there. And I fact, when in the past it came down to verifying that I'm really me, I mentioned to other people that I am a book author and that they could verify my identity through my books, at a book presentation or when I have a public interview.

Curiously, nobody ever considered any of that as evidence that I'm really me... very curiously, only *Instagram* counts for them!

4- Apart from the woman discussed here, I did talk to some other people, too. The most notable is the person from "message proposal 23", a 24 year old woman from Zambia who literally provided men with a self-rating system in her profile. You can read more about her, and everyone else involved in this entire research, in the first annex to this book.

==========

8- What's next?

I was led to all this research because, when I first created a profile that seemed to perfectly capture my spirit and who I really am, nobody was interested in that person. Over a week, my completely real profile only got 30 likes, half of them completely false ones, and absolutely no introductory messages. Then, when I created a profile that still captured a small part of my spirit and who I really am, and replaced my original photos with beautifully false ones, suddenly I mattered, and not only did I received 2343 "likes" in a week, but 184 people even decided to message me first. And this is extremely disappointing, almost hurtful, not because I could be specially ugly or lack any self-confidence – remember the nature of the six photos I initially picked, they were not picked because I looked specially attractive in any of them, but simply for the fact they represented multiple aspects of my being – but for the fact that people are now self-boycotting their own happiness.

For example, think about the person behind

"message proposal 13", a 39 year old single parent from Oeiras, Portugal. I had originally contacted her in my first profile, over that one major issue I spotted there, but never got an answer back from her. When I created the second one, and in spite of its nature still being the same as the previous', not only was she now interested in talking to me, but even messaged me first. The lesson to be learned here is a very simple one – in online dating nobody seems to care about who you are, or any of your accomplishments, unless you provide them with beautiful photos, which matter way more than your past, present and future. Without that pretty square in your profile, your entire existence is soon made completely irrelevant; with one, you're then quickly elevated to the most amazing man who has lived – and, in fact, nobody wanted to talk to me, the author, in my original profile, but in the second one people suddenly started asking about my books.

The whole idea makes me want to puke, it truly makes me feel horrible, because people could be meeting truly amazing individuals, ones which could genuinely add a lot to their lives, and instead, by repeatedly focusing on all the wrong things, they are left broken and alone, without ever contemplating the idea that they are going at it all wrong.

Comparing and contrasting this whole thing with our daily lives, can you imagine how it would feel if a woman just wanted to go out with a man when he has a beard? Or, if you're a woman, can you imagine how it would feel to be told something along the lines of "I want to go out with you, but only after you have lost some 20 kg"? It would be an utter absurdity, and yet it is also one that is becoming tacitly accepted on a daily basis in the virtual context of online dating, where people's true personalities and all their personal achievements are now seen as irrelevant, while an absurd culture based exclusively on static pictures of idealized realities is constantly being fostered.

But... there is actually a real solution, although I find it highly unlikely any major company will ever implement it. In the past I have read some peer reviewed studies which present the idea that a perfect online dating experience can be created by joining two people together and have them share a common online experience, such as walking (virtually) through a museum while discussing what they are both seeing. Such an idea not only reveals who both people truly are, but also fosters a realistic common ground to connect over. And it seems to have generated great results, in test conditions, but... when you really think about it, the reason why this is not implemented by any big companies becomes obvious – deep inside, online dating is not really about promoting good relationships, or about helping us all find a genuine person for our lives, but about wasting people's time while repeatedly selling them the illusion that by doing it again and again, as mice stuck in a wheel, we may eventually get a different result.

But, in a very unsettling way, when I eventually created one final test profile to spot potential patterns in initial messages, I found out that some people were contacting wholly different users with precisely the same initial messages, regardless of the content of the readers' respective profiles. This further exacerbates the absurd repetitiveness of the process, and that for people creating those apps and websites we are all nothing more than mice in a wheel, addicted to an enormous fantasy – which is frequently promoted in their advertised "success stories" – that if we try it enough times, one day we will actually be able to find what we seek. Oddly, they even seem to acknowledge this whole problem by constantly proposing to their users the acquisition of premium subscriptions of multiple months, tacitly admitting something along the lines of "you'll be here for long and you still won't find what you seek".

But if you're still not convinced, perhaps a message I received from *Bumble*'s Customer Support in 2022 will prove you so – when I contacted them with a fairly simple question[12], a phrase present in their answer astonished me, "Our records show that profiles with clear, original photos receive *more matches*, and *we're sure this is exactly what you want!*" At first I assumed this was just a random employee, Chloe, unintentionally saying a very significative thing, but just a day later a second support member, Noah, concluded his own answer with the same sentence, and eventually a higher-level employee, Esther, even further elaborated on the same idea, showing this exact phrase is actually a set part of

---

12 For more information, check "Annex 7".

their internal processes – i.e. the idea that all users want *more matches*, not *better ones* or *actually meeting someone*. One would think people were joining their app for the latter, not just to waste their time scrolling through photos and getting matches, but when I confronted their press division with this intriguing statement from their own staff, they neither confirmed *nor denied* this is their internal policy. Such direct failure to deny the whole idea confirms they do believe people join them for the rush of getting more and more matches (and that those are always derived directly from photos), while endlessly spinning the aforementioned wheel, and that the "dating" part is, in itself, completely secondary.

And, in fact, the actual experience in online dating reported across this book indeed proves this whole point. I conducted the second part of this whole experience for a week, to a total of 7x24x60 = 10080 minutes. During that period of time, 2343 people liked my profile, roughly one person every four minutes – and this is in almost-ideal conditions, with falsely alluring photos being presented to people. Out of those, only 184 decided to message me first. From that number, only 11 of them seemed interesting enough for me to talk to. And, finally, out of them, *zero* proved to be interested enough to really want to talk to me, instead abandoning the conversations we were having as if we both had all the time in the world to resume them later. And so, I wasted two weeks of my own time in the fantasy of online dating, so you hopefully won't have to do it yourself.

===== Curiosities =====

1- If you've read this book up to now, chances are that you're extremely curious about what three apps and websites I was using for this experiment. I can openly disclose that one of them was *Bumble*, even due to usage of some of its information on the annexes, but I cannot reveal the remaning ones, for legal and privacy reasons. However, I can openly admit that I simply picked the three biggest ones I could find, to ensure that my personal experience was one that is shared, on a daily basis, by many other men.

2- An interesting, and yet largely unknown, aspect of online dating apps is that they slightly change the user's experience based on their current location. For example, when I changed mine to Japan, I was then asked to confirm my age with a legal document; for the US, my profiles were added many additional options, such as the ability to display my opinion on abortion; for Iran, due to totally unknown reasons an app became very slow and appeared to malfunction; and potential listings of your main interests tend to vary widely from country to country, among many other local changes!

3- Although, as far as I know, the innovative idea of online dating presented in this chapter still isn't available in a live environment, you may be able to accomplish similar results by enrolling in virtual online experiences with other people, such as using *Second Life* or playing *World of Warcraft*. I never tested any of the two, but their underlying concept may provide you with a shared experience similar to the one described above.

4- A notable search engine query appears to ask

about the success rate of particular online dating apps and websites. Although I can readily grant that some may have more success for particular users than others, one should realize that in the test conditions reported through these chapters the success rate for the three biggest and most famous services of the genre appears to be under 1%, potentially even 0%, across 2343 people who "liked" my second profile. And, in a real environment, would you consider going out on dates with over two thousand people to meet the man or woman of your life? I know I wouldn't, but to each his own.

5- The main content of this book ends here, but you may also want to check at least the first annex, where all the data collected for this research is presented. Who knows, you may even get to laugh a bit over what people say in their profiles and how they approached me on their own!

==========

ANNEX 1 – Data collected

Message proposal 1 – 28 years old, Campo Grande, Brazil[13]

"Hey there! Nice meeting you! Let me introduce my self a little. I am Brazilian, 7 day Adventist, 28 years, I take faith too serious! Looking for my future husband, not for fun at all! Just message back if you think we could match"[14]

Six photos, one of them so badly edited that she looked as thin as a living skeleton. Had this person read my profile at all? I felt she hadn't, because not only was she messaging someone in Portugal in slightly broken English, when we both speak almost the same language, but her profile, and her introduction, stated almost exclusively the same information, i.e. she is very religious and she wants a serious relationship. Nothing wrong in either of those two wishes, of course, but why was she messaging me at all? Not only does she not tell me, but she ends her message

---

13 Across all the proposals presented here, some of the biographical information was slightly changed for privacy reasons.

14 This, and all initial messages that people sent to me, are here reproduced precisely as I received them. No typos were corrected, but for messages in non-English languages I tried to provide an approximate translation of the original content.

with "message back if you think we could match", i.e. contact me if we're both seeking the same, almost as if she was simply sending that same message in bulk to many other people.

Message proposal 2 – 33, Salvador, Brazil

"Hi [my name here]. How are you?"

Just a generic message. Particularly interesting, and worthy of note, is the fact she had a total of ten photos in her profile, and yet only two words of text – "Ask me" – an expression which, as previously discussed, is a typical indicative of a very low-effort profile.

Message proposal 3 – 34, Brasília, Brazil

"🖤"

Again, just a generic message, with close to no effort. She had six photos in her profile, but nothing there said anything even significative about who she is, with the exception of she stating that her current goal was "surviving bolsominions and bolsonaro ♡", i.e. a political-related assertion. Perhaps as oddly, random sections of her profile were in English, while others were written in her native Portuguese.

Message proposal 4 – 36, Tucson, Arizona, US

"Hi"

Zero-effort message. Six photos, but just four lines of profile information, which were started with an almost generic "all my life is about God, justice, love, music, dance, chess and holism."

Message proposal 5 – 43, San José, Costa Rica

"How is everything ☺"

Yet again, a zero-effort message. Four photos in her profile, with she presenting herself with the following words – "Alegre, dinámica, disfruto de lo simple de la vida. ☺", i.e. "joyful, dynamic, I enjoy the simple things in life".

Message proposal 6 – 31, Manila, Philippines

"Hi!! :)"

Profile with six photos, where she simply introduces herself with the following words "Not here for hook ups. Not here for kinky conversations." One definitely has to wonder if she used to get *that* many requests for hook ups and "kinky conversations" (whatever that means), because she says literally nothing else about herself.

Message proposal 7 – 46, Bangkok, Thailand

"Not really into the online stuff either... but given where I'm currently working, my choices are limited. And so here I am, looking for someone who is worth traveling for, and maybe even relocating for..."

This profile featured 10 photos, was filled with information about her, and she actually seems to have read the limited information provided in mine, interacting with it a little bit and even suggesting that our physical distance may not be a problem for her at all. Featuring all of this is a good idea overall, and in the end I even ended up replying to her message. Later, she ended up messaging a second test profile, in which she again interacted with the actual content, proving that this lady was paying attention to the content of everyone's profiles.

Message proposal 8 – 35, Malang, Indonesia

"Hope we can be a good friend 😊"

10 photos, but a single line of text, "i'm caring..loyal..crazy sometimes". Taking into account the generic message she sent me, plus the fact she literally decided to describe herself as "crazy", one definitely has to wonder how desperate a man would need to be in order to interact with her. But a significant question did stay in my mind – does

she just go around and propose to become "good friends" with everyone? We'll never know...

Message proposal 9 – 29, Changi Village, Singapore

"Hey"

A profile with six photos, three of them in what seem to be her local mountains, explaining why her profile contains the words "#mountains", among a few irrelevant others. She also claims to be looking for a serious relationship, and yet tells people little about herself besides "I love eating and culinary". Perhaps this profile would have intrigued me a bit, but at the same time she made very little effort to talk to me.

Message proposal 10 – 34, Labuhanbajo, Indonesia

"Hi [my name here],. I love you smile😍"

In this one case, the reason why she contacted me is extremely obvious – the photos, and the photos alone, of which she herself has only four. At the same time, she mentions her *Instagram* username in her profile, and when I checked it she had 58 publications but 1065 followers (and following 697). And yet, she claims to be looking for a serious relationship. One definitely has to wonder if she expects to find it just among pretty photos, instead of with real human beings...

Message proposal 11 – 30, Coro, Philippines
"Hi adorable puppy you had😊😊"

This profile almost made me puke. It had some significant information through multiple of its sections, to a total of about 300 words, but it also presented 16 selfies of her – 10 in the photo section, and six others across her text section – along with an enormous number of emojis. She is clearly obsessed with her own self-image, which is never a good thing.

Message proposal 12 – 32, Denpasar, Indonesia
"Hi [my name here]. Youre a great package! Would you wait for me to save up for a euro trip together? 😅"

Three photos. Why am I even "a great package", if she knows close to nothing about me? And, at the same time, knowing close to nothing about her, why would I wait for her to (eventually) travel to Europe? For the simple fact she is female? For God's sake...

Message proposal 13 – 39, Oeiras, Portugal

"Olá. Como estás?" [i.e. "Hi. How are you?"]

Seemingly a single parent trying to restart dating again. Absolutely nothing wrong with that, if it wasn't for the fact one of her six photos featured text in which she advised *all* men to invest more in their mental health. This kind of profile, fortunately very rare, where people try to educate others about some kind of cause, always makes me wonder if they consider themselves so above regular mankind that everyone else is completely imperfect to them. Why would I, why would anyone, ever want to meet a girl who says little about herself, and yet already considers that all men have serious mental health problems?

Message proposal 14 – 36, Jakarta, Indonesia

"Hello [my name here] 😊"

Another message with close to no effort at all. At least she filled part of the profile, and had seven selfies there.

Message proposal 15 – 38, Manila, Philippines

"Hi [my name here]! I don't know if you'll ever get to read this but I hope you do. 😁"

Ten photos, and sure, I did read her message, but... what

for? I went on to read her full profile and, strangely, it was actually a good one, where she provided plenty of information about herself, from what she seeks ("Looking for someone who knows how to have a good conversation. Someone who actually cares enough to know that conversations have to be two-way."), to her religion ("I am a Christian and my faith is very important to me. Looking for someone who wants a God-honoring relationship."), and even some of the things she enjoys (e.g. "I love to travel and experience sunrises and sunsets in every place that I explore.") Perhaps I would have contacted her back, but I feel the content of her initial message, here, did way more harm than good.

Message proposal 16 – 44, Jakarta, Indonesia
"Hi"

Six badly edited photos. Perhaps one of the most desperate profiles I had found until now, the one of a single mother who even writes down that she wants "to be happy the rest of my life with u . yess Uuuu 🥰😍😭😭". Would she say this to literally every man? Is she willing to settle for anyone who is just the opposite gender? It baffled me.

Message proposal 17 – 39, 广州, China
"So cute puppy"

Six photos, in which she even provides the dates from when they were taken. The strange thing here is that this one girl from China had a very complete profile, and yet contacted me over the puppy photo alone. I would perhaps have written her back, because she tells the reader a lot about herself and also tried to interact with the content of my own profile.

Message proposal 18 – 36, Otista, Indonesia
"Hi"

A single parent with a completely empty profile but 10 photos, and with zero effort in her message. Why would I answer back, unless I was going for looks alone?

Message proposal 19 – 46, Manila, Philippines
"hi [my name here]! have i spelled your name right? or should it be spelled C-U-T-I-E 😊"

Four photos. When I first read this message, a complete blank hit me. I was absolutely baffled. Perhaps I would have expected such a thing from a young teen, but this was an older woman, a single parent, who claims that one of her current goals is "to finally find a man i can call my own. where are you hiding? why are you so difficult to find? 😳".

What could I say, at all? I'm not even sure, except for the fact that I would usually not answer her at all – and, in fact, she seems to say similar things to everyone, with a message she sent to a different test profile instead reading: "hi [my name here]! have i spelled your name right? or should it be spelled A-M-A-Z-I-N-G-L-Y C-U-T-I-E 😁".

Message proposal 20 – 48, Kebagusan, Indonesia
"Hai there"

Close to zero effort on her side. Her profile had 10 photos, and yet all she says, supposedly about herself, is "I need someone to love me, and caring and faithful and no bullshit cause i dont have time with someone like that, go away for cheater or scammer", followed by her *Instagram* username. It only gets stranger if we consider that she had literal horns in one of her photos.

Message proposal 21 – 19, Dar es Salaam, Tanzania
"Hi"

A really strange profile. She had nine photos, but every single section of her writing insisted exclusively on the fact she is looking for a serious relationship. It was not just a copy-paste, she literally went through the trouble of finding different ways to constantly mention that in every section. One definitely has to wonder why, given the fact she did not seem like an unattractive woman at all – chances are that she usually displays as little effort in her past relationships as she did in the message she sent me?!

Message proposal 22 – 28, Bandung, Indonesia
"Hi"

Four photos. She describes herself simply as "a warm, loyal, sincerely, loving, with a sweet personality 😊". That's literally all we get to know about her, perhaps along with the fact she puts zero effort in her messages.

Message proposal 23 – 24, Lusaka, Zambia
"Hello, How are you doing? I'm [her name here], I would like to get to know you, that's if you don't mind. If you are feeling unmotivated, who or what helps you get yourself going?"

10 photos. When I read her message, the final question seemed a bit out of place, as if she just wanted to ask a completely random thing. Maybe she does it to everyone? I was curious, and so I went to read her profile, where I

found one of the craziest things I have ever seen in an
online dating profile. Given its nature, it deserves to be
quoted in full here:

"1. If you are a Christian +15

2. If you prioritize family +8

3. Self confident +5

4. Honest +7

5. Have a kind heart +11

6. Emotionally intelligent +6

7. Appreciate little things +12

8. Can cook +4

9. If you can take responsibility of your behavior/actions +5

10. If you are a good listener +11

11. If you are patient +8

12. Hardworking +8

ROUND TWO ☺

1. Not Religious -20

2. Prideful/Bossy -10

3. Lack patience -4

4. Don't value family and friendship -15

5. Don't plan or keep commitments -8

6. Emotionally closed off -6

7. Short tempered -4

8. If you smoke -6

9. Can't hold a conversation -7

10. Alcoholic -4

11. Not Hardworking -9

12. Have low self-esteem -7

IF YOUR SCORE IS LESS THAN 80 PLEASE DON'T BOTHER TEXTING, LETS NOT WASTE EACH OTHERS TIME,THANK YOU☺"

This one woman is literally asking men to consider a score system based on which she will see if they are worthy of that immense honour of talking to her or not. And so, unlike in hundreds of other cases stated here, I decided to actually send her a message on the side, as soon as possible, attempting to find out what would happen if, in spite of her initial message, I purposely showed myself not to possess any of the characteristics she rates as positive above. Unfortunately, I never got to that point, but what happened is still fascinating – she repeatedly showed zero interest in actually holding a real conversation, until I eventually got tired of it and stopped talking to her. And this definitely confirms the broad vision she paints in her profile – she considers herself so much better than everyone else that she can afford to make little effort in even holding any real conversations with anyone. So, if you ever find a profile like this, one that rates other human beings as far as literally assigning points to their possible characteristics, the message couldn't be clearer – stay away!

Message proposal 24 – 32, Jakarta, Indonesia

"Hi! How are u doing?"

Her profile had eight photos, but it is her personal description of herself that most deserves being noted here - "I like aviation. I'm looking for serious relationship. No drama, please!" So, if you're that *super unusual* person who also likes aviation, you've probably met your match; if you're not, well, this is all there is to her, and absolutely nothing else.

Message proposal 25 – 36, Camp Phillips, Philippines

"Hi"

10 photos, but if one of the dreams of your life is knowing, from the get-go, how problematic dating a specific woman would be, your dream may come true with this profile. The very first thing she says is, and I quote, "Honestly I'm married, but still processing my legal separation. I have kid, he is now 13 years old. My estranged husband left us 2 years ago. He is an OFW working in Japan for more than 4 years already. But unfortunately he left us all of the sudden. With what happened to my love story, I am still moving

forward – fixing myself and take courage to stand still for my child." So, if you want a potentially problematic woman in your life, this is it – me, I'd rather skip it.

Message proposal 26 – 40, Wloclawek, Poland

"Hey, how are you doing? Sending you a hug as its the perfect gift, its free and can be easily returned ☺"

Six photos, including one of a meme with Snoopy. Hers was a potentially interesting approach, but when I went to read her profile, it said absolutely nothing about herself, instead being filled with some very vague and completely stereotypical wisdom phrases, such as "Be yourself no matter what they say". And, in fact, later she send this exact same initial message to another test profile.

Message proposal 27 – 26, Nairobi, Kenya

"[My name here] my friend insisted i give it a try tooo hahaha our friends hate seeing us single"

She had a very complete profile, along with five photos. And yet, she clearly read my profile. I did write her back, mostly because she does talk about herself across her profile sections.

Message proposal 28 – 40, Jakarta, Indonesia
"Hola como estas?" [i.e. "Hello how are you?"]

By mere coincidence, given the comment above, next I found this other profile. It featured a single photo, where she is barely seen, and presents herself as a "simple person, love travelling". But why was she even writing me in Spanish? We'll never know.

Message proposal 29 – 28, San Francisco, Philippines
"Hi."

Six photos, in yet another person displaying zero effort. Although she filled most of her profile sections, they were all very simple and featured nothing specially informative.

Message proposal 30 – 44, Quezon City, Philippines
"Yeah you should online dating. Who knows it might be me you're looking for 😍"

Four selfies, and only tells readers that she's "a warm-hearted person, sensitive, love cats and dogs". At the same time, she also claims she is looking for "a serious relationship only". Whether she did read my profile, or not, is a bit dubious, but she seemed a bit desperate, to the point she mentioned her e-mail address and her *Instagram* username on her profile (533 publications, 380 followers, following 1152).

Message proposal 31 – 39, Makati, Philippines
"Hello"

Her zero effort is only further exacerbated by her profile content – a single photo of Planet Earth, and some text that went "Just checking things out here." Why would I, why would anyone, ever write her back?

Message proposal 32 – 33, Surabaya, Indonesia
"Hello, how are you?"

Very similar to the previous one, except this one has four photos of landscapes and provides some description of herself, i.e. "an easy making friend person, hard working, a honest person". But, again, given this whole lot of information she provides, why would anyone write to her?

Message proposal 33 – 37, Manila, Philippines
"Hello"

Yet another one who follows the same scheme – zero effort, a single photo, and the text "Simple Person want simple life". She even approached another test profile with this exact same initial message!

Message proposal 34 – 44, Batangas, Philippines
"hi"

Two photos of herself, "Simple gurl☺". At the time, I was even starting to wonder if most women in the Philippines being this low-effort was a known issue...

Message proposal 35 – 47, Makati, Philippines
"Cute dog! Yours?"

Overall, this person had a well-written profile, where she tells people about herself and her needs, plus seven photos (although she openly admitted that some of them were outdated and over two years old). Given her honesty and the fact she commented on the (limited) content of my profile, I would possibly write her back.

Message proposal 36 – 36, Surabaya, Indonesia
"Hi, [my name here] What's ur fave bucket list?"

One photo. I didn't even understand what she was trying to ask me, but even if I had, I wouldn't write her back. Why? Essentially, due to the way she presents herself in her profile – she literally just tells potential readers that "I'm proud to be Moslem also Mom of 3kids". There's absolutely nothing wrong with either of those two things, but she should also tell people more about her.

Message proposal 37 – 36, Dusseldorf, Germany
"Cute"

Four photos. Something seemed fishy about this profile, until I noticed what was going on – this person was actually from Thailand, but she simply changed her location to a country from Europe. Meanwhile, being called "cute" is not exactly a good way to start a conversation, unless the guy on the other side of the screen is quite a desperate one...

Message proposal 38 – 38, Montreal, Quebec, Canada
" "

Three photos. Another similar case, "Currently, I live in Jakarta, Indonesia. I change my location to get more matches 😁". When a person literally admits to be pulling such a scheme just to get more attention on her, why should you even give it to her?

Message proposal 39 – 37, Port Moresby, Papua New Guinea

"Hello I'm [her name here] from Papua New Guinea"

So... the information she provides in her initial message is literally the one you can already read in her basic profile. In addition to that, she only tells you that she is "Simple,kind, humble and honest", and that "Sunday is the most perfect day". With two photos, plus a picture of a famous quote, what real reason is there to talk to her, unless you really want to meet someone from Papua New Guinea?

Message proposal 40 – 30, Davao, Philippines

"Hi [my name here]. How are you doing?"

A profile with six photos, mostly of her doing things, but sometimes with her face hidden. And yet, her profile – with a total of six lines of text – talked about herself in a very general sense, from "sincere and very easy to talk to" to "I love God" and "my passion is loving the Lord". I understand people may be very faithful, but what about telling the reader more about who they are?

Message proposal 41 – 37, Santo Domingo, Dominican Republic

"Hello hadsome 😊😊"

Regardless of the evident typo in the initial message, this single parent described herself in a noteworthy way - "I have long straight hair, I am chubby, mestiza, I consider myself a beautiful woman both on the outside and on the inside. I don't want superficial people." One certainly has to wonder why, if she doesn't want superficial people, she talks so much about her own physicality, has a single photo in her profile, and refers to me based exclusively on my physical element. Double standards?

Message proposal 42 – 40, Varna, Bulgaria

"That look speaks volumes:)"

Almost predictably by now, this profile had nine photos (including a very sexy bikini one), but "described" herself with a single phrase - "Be too much of a lady to put up with anything less than a gentleman". What this is supposed to mean is a bit unclear, but regardless of its significance, she does not say anything real about herself. As such, her focus on just my photos seems to become a bit more tolerable...

Message proposal 43 – 34, Cebu City, Philippines

"Hi [my name *with a typo*]. You wanna give a try knowing each other?"

Seven photos. She barely described anything significant about herself in her profile – "one of a kind, simple, loving caring and kind" – but what makes this profile specially noteworthy is a somewhat long rant she also presents in it – "I'm looking for someone that I can have a funny and serious conversation with. Someone who's searching for his other half to be his future wife 😊. I know guys here are very picky and have its own standard. Mostly, they are proactive to response to those girls which has sexy profile pics on it. 😄 Am I right? Well, If I message you that means I want to build a connection with you, means I like to know u and talk to you, but sad fact I didn't get any response from them 😊. Do I have to post my sexy pics?? Hell no!! 😅 I'm not that desperate😅. Anyways, you can freely send me a message if your that guy that I'm looking for..."
Oh, if only she had such a passion for saying anything real about who she is, maybe more people would want to get to know her...

Message proposal 44 – 43, Jakarta, Indonesia
"Hi"

This was a bit of a strange profile, with one of her six

photos even presenting some sort of religious quote in Indonesian. It only gets worse if you try to read it – she says absolutely nothing about herself, instead just directing people to her *Instagram* username (588 publications, 491 followers, following 198).

Message proposal 45 – 27, Makati, Philippines
"Whats your research title?"

A pretty basic profile, with five photos (including one of a beautiful sunset), and a single word, "catmum". At least she seems to have read my profile, but unless I was a super huge cat lover – and I'm not – what other reasons would I even have to talk to her?

Message proposal 46 – 29, Davao, Philippines
"Hi there [my name here] 😊"

Profile with just three photos (including an almost-sexual one), and simply a reference to an *Instagram* username. Funnily, when I tried to check it, the account she alludes to didn't even exist any more!

Message proposal 47 – 32, Tarlac, Philippines
"Hello there stranger!"

Five photos. Yet another profile which seems to be used to advertise an *Instagram* username (hers had 45 publications, 218 followers and following 376). She says close to nothing in her profile, besides the odd fact that she likes ping pong. I feel her own words describe it best when she says "I'm just looking around and see where it goes."

Message proposal 48 – 26, Laguna, Philippines
"Hi!"

Four photos. This profile deserves to be noted for its profound irony – she doesn't say anything significative about herself, but her literal first paragraph says, and I quote, "So tired of HI's and Hellos. Come on guys, you're in dating app don't be shy and stop feeling awkward. Give me your best pick up lines ;)" And yet, she herself makes the exact same thing she appears to criticize in others...

Message proposal 49 – 28, Manila, Philippines
"what's in your bucket list if you can share :)"

Nine photos. One more "honest and kind person" who says absolutely nothing else about herself, but does mention her *Instagram name* in her profile, instead of her *username* (which is a lot more common and seemingly easier to find).

I did not even bother looking it up.

Message proposal 50 – 37, Pekayon, Philippines

"Hi portugal ᴘᴛ Christiano Ronaldo"

Six photos. This woman was "sigle" [sic]. Besides that, she says absolutely nothing else about her, with the exclusion of her *Instagram* username (45 publications, 477 followers, following 829). At the same time, it is interesting to note she mentions the country I'm supposedly in, but writes the name of the famous football player wrong.

Message proposal 51 – 43, Tamarindo, Costa Rica

"I just stopped to your profile..."

This profile had nine photos, and it was also very well filled in each of its sections. I would probably write back to it, perhaps because I did not even understand what she had tried to say in her initial message.

Message proposal 52 – 38, Jakarta, Indonesia

"Hi [my name here].. Nice to meet you. ✨"

Out of this person's seven photos, five of them were in a

gym. Cumulatively, she says a single thing in her profile, "162cm". Why would I write it back, unless I myself was also a complete gym addict?

Message proposal 53 – 43, León, Mexico

"Hi [my name here]! Nice profile 😉"

I would certainly take her own "nice profile" much more seriously if it wasn't for the fact that, as you may recall, my profile was almost empty, barring six photos and two small paragraphs of text. Oddly, this lady had six photos in hers, and claims to have visited 30 different countries, but says nothing else besides the evident fact that she likes travelling.

Message proposal 54 – 32, Manila, Philippines

"Hi [my name here]! I'm [her name here] from Philippines, I'm also new here and same with you may family and friends push me to try this app. By the way I just want you to know that I'm interested and would like to get to know you."

As you can easily see, this person sent me a very complete message. Her profile was also extensive filled, featured 10 photos from completely different places, and, when mentioning she likes dogs, even presented a photo of herself with what is supposedly her pet. I would possibly have written her back, if it wasn't for the fact she was using a clearly fake name in her account, and then approached me with a completely different one, which is always very fishy.

Message proposal 55 – 33, Medan, Indonesia
"bi"

Three photos, and absolutely no information besides "I'm Mom of two kids 😊". I have absolutely no idea on what she even meant by her attempt at an initial message.

Message proposal 56 – 25, Panamá, Panama
"Hi"

Zero effort on her initial message. However, the reasons here are quite easy to understand – she had three super sexy photos, very limited profile text, and when she mentions her *Instagram* username, she has 120 publications, 1998 followers and is following 703 people. She is clearly used up to being approached by completely "thirsty" men, and so she probably feels that there's no need to ever make an effort to talk to people. So, why talk to someone who makes so little effort in presenting who she is, as an actual human being? Just because she is not exactly ugly and presents herself as a very sexual being...? Thanks, but no.

Message proposal 57 – 39, General Santos, Philippines

"Hello how are you?"

10 photos, but all she tells people about herself is "I am single and no kids", along with "I am loyal, honest, responsible, kind and down to earth". Who would ever say the opposite? Anyone at all?!

Message proposal 58 – 27, Mexico City, Mexico

"Hey"

A profile with four photos, and where the owner says nothing else about herself besides "Looking for a genuine connection". At times like these, I cannot help but wondering why people would approach this kind of profile, even more since "a genuine connection" is extremely hard to achieve when you know nothing about the person.

Message proposal 59 – 40, Jakarta, Indonesia

"Perfect"

What can I even say, by now, to yet another profile that features six photos (one of them with a meme), but absolutely nothing about herself, apart from "I'm an ordinary woman with big heart and big dream ♡"?

Message proposal 60 – 38, Spring, Texas, US
"Nice"

Nine photos and a whopping 3200 words in her profile may seem very impressive, until you realize that her selected name is "Marriage Only". Meaning, she is specifically and only looking for a guy who marries her... which could be reasonable, until you realize that the best she has to offer, when it comes to seeing your own profile, is a single word. Why she remains single, given her enormous wish for a marriage (and, all things considered, I genuinely fear for the guy who ends up marrying her under these conditions), is hardly difficult to understand.

Message proposal 61 – 24, Danao, Philippines
"hi"

Six photos, most of them being attempts at looking sexy. And then, what does she tell you about her? "a single mother of a boy" and "looking for a guy who can be a father to my son, not just hook ups". As any reasonable person may easily understand, presenting all kinds of sexy photos is hardly the best way to go searching for what she desires...

Message proposal 62 – 29, Bangkok, Thailand

"Hii you look gentle with the dog"

Obviously, she contacted me over one of my photos. Three regular photos, one of her topless in the beach (!), and all we get to hear from her is "A Thai girl who has stopped drinking since 2017". Great for her, but what else does she have to offer? It seems nobody will ever know.

Message proposal 63 – 29, Davao, Philippines

"yay! adorable dog 😊 what is his/her name?"

A bit of a strange profile, in the sense she has 10 photos, but each of the five pairs was taken in the exact same place but with a completely different pose. Some are a bit sexy. The profile has some information on her, particularly saying she is going to undertake a PhD and she is currently a mental health care professional. She also mentions her *Instagram* username (102 publications, 845 followers, following 79). Given all these, and the fact she did try to interact with me based on my profile content, I would probably write her back.

Message proposal 64 – 24, Laguna, Philippines

"Heyyy nice to know you here 😁"

One more profile with eight photos, but which tells very little about her – nothing besides "hope to find a serious one" and "I'm kind i don't bite unless you like 😊". Thanks, but no.

Message proposal 65 – 30, Manila, Philippines

"♡"

Following the same trend, she has 10 photos in her profile but doesn't even bother telling people anything about her besides that she is looking for a "serious relationship". Given this extreme lack of effort, why would I even consider answering her back?

Message proposal 66 – 39, Bangkok, Thailand

"Hi"

Three photos, from a woman who briefly describes herself as "simple woman who is warm and sweet heart" and "Open mind to meeting a man that has children, but I am not open to scammer". It definitely sounds a bit weird to say this – I mean, did a woman ever feel she would be okay with meeting a scammer? – but the fact she says nothing significant about who she is, that's certainly a much bigger deal for me.

Message proposal 67 – 42, Cluj-Napoca, Romania

"Hello 👋"

This one had three photos, in none of which you can even see her face, but at least she gives us some basic information about who she is – "Idealist, dreamer, sociable, genuine, adventurous, thinker, passionate, creative". I still wouldn't talk to her, but at least a potential reader is given *something* to work with.

Message proposal 68 – 33, Aguascalientes, Mexico

"Hello there"

When a profile has eight photos of a woman in gym-related environments, and yet all she has to say is "I wanna give this site a chance let's make some friends", what are you even supposed to talk to her about, besides the fact she goes to the gym?

Message proposal 69 – 33, Quezon City, Philippines

"Heloo"

This one got to the absurdity of featuring six photos, in none of which you can see her face, and then redirecting people to her *Instagram* username, where she has 131 publications, 122 followers and is following 339 people. This really seems like just trying to advertise your social media and *failing* in that goal...

Message proposal 70 – 29, Istanbul, Turkey

"Hey"

Once more, 10 photos, but all you get to know about her is "I'm just a simple girl" and "looking for serious relationship". Unless you go for looks and nothing else, why would you even talk to her, given her notable lack of effort?

Message proposal 71 – 29, Seseh, Indonesia

"Hi"

A profile with five photos and an *Instagram* username (33 publications, 1124 followers, following 561), but which says nothing else about herself. Strangely, her photos seem overly posed, as if she had taken them at a studio.

Message proposal 72 – 25, Baao, Philippines
"Hey"

Five photos at the beach, one of them a bit sexy, but regarding herself all you get is "i am kind, loyal, and god fearing". This last expression, "god fearing", seems to also appear in many other profiles, mostly ones from Kenya, and when asked about it, people eventually explained to me that it simply means "Christian".

Message proposal 73 – 25, Palu, Indonesia
"hi"

When I think I've already seen many things, this profile suddenly appeared – three selfies, and just the text "Mencintai dengan sederhana 🪶", which is clearly Indonesian. What that really means is perhaps secondary over the fact she doesn't say much about her.

Message proposal 74 – 30, Bajarmasin, Indonesia
"I like your profile, may I know more about you?"

Ten photos, but yet one more time all you get to know

about her is, and it deserves to be quoted, "Trying my luck on this app, to find Mr.The Right One". Good goal, one could argue, but what do we even know about her? Nothing...

Message proposal 75 – 25, Birigui, Brazil

"Olá, fiquei curiosa sobre ser autor, eu adoro ler e quero saber, que tipo de livros você escreve?" [i.e. "Hi, I was curious about you being an author, I love reading and I want to know, what kind of books do you write?"]

In this particular case, she clearly read the little text available in my profile. Then, when I checked her profile, it all started to make sense – she has three photos (two of them in some kind of religious function, also two where she appears with a ton of makeup), literally starts her profile with a mention to her *Instagram* username (97 publications, 968 followers, following 734, and even contains the text "Christian"), and claims she wants "to meet someone for a lifelong relationship." It is perfectly okay to want any of this, as always, and she even said a little bit about herself and what she likes, but... there is a bit of a funny thing regarding all this, which is the fact that in my real profile, *nobody* ever approached me over me being an author. Instead, with this new profile, suddenly the fact I write started mattering, with people repeatedly asking me the exact same question, the one she also asked her, which is theoretically a very simple way to start a conversation with me. Maybe I would have answered her, but I'm not too sure about it, mostly due to the fact that an overly religious woman is often dangerous, as she tends to compare her suitors to fictitiously high ideals which are really very hard to achieve.

Message proposal 76 – 29, Bang Kapi, Thailand

"hi"

10 photos. Zero effort on her initial message, which here kind of makes a bit of sense - "sorry i can speak eng. just a little bit". So, unable to speak much English, she instead just gives people a broad listing of her likes – "motorcycles, cooking, exercising, running, traveling, forests, mountains, beaches, camping, hiking, coffee, animals, IT." Oddly enough, she also mentions her *Instagram* username in her profile (1361 publications, 1736 followers, 1758 following), and there she provides the exact same text in precisely the same order. Chances are that she doesn't even speak real English, and so, how would one even be able to talk to her?!

Message proposal 77 – 31, Frankfurt am Main, Germany

"Hi [my name here]. How are you?"

Five photos. A profile that starts literally with the lines "Please read: I am not in this location. I just change location for this app. I am currently in philippines." is always a hassle, even more when she doesn't even provide a real reason why she changed her location. It only gets weirder – although she writes 260 words in her profile, she doesn't say anything significative, instead sticking to broad statements, which probably apply to everyone, such as "I do have my own uniqueness."

Message proposal 78 – 33, Bogo, Philippines
"Hello"

Ten photos, all of them seemingly taken in attractions from the Philippines, including one with her sitting by a tiger. And then, you try to read the profile, and... all she says about her is that "my work allows me to travel", perhaps to hint at the fact she may be able to potentially meet guys elsewhere.

Message proposal 79 – 38, Jakarta, Indonesia
"Hi"

A single photo, strangely crowded with ads at the top and bottom of her face, which was apparently taken from another app. A single line in her profile, "iam mature woman need good friend". Why would anyone ever approach her on any of this?!

Message proposal 80 – 30, Cilandak, Indonesia
"Hi [my name here]….."

Four photos, in one of which she looks sick or potentially drunk. Then, all her text profile is "Hii…", giving you the hint that you can just skip it.

Message proposal 81 – 28, Bindoy, Philippines
"hiii… wanna talk to a Filipina?"

Nine photos, including an attempt at a sexy one in a swimming pool, and one with a super sexy night shirt, where she is also wearing a Covid-19 mask. It gets much weirder, by the time you read the profile – "if you can treat her right, you're definitely the lucky one", "she doesn't need a man who doesn't need her", "I easily get jealous", "don't search or look other girls behind my back", plus a goal of "Meeting the man who would take care of me"… this is clearly a profile catering to desperate English men who are looking for the proverbial mail order bride from the Philippines, and hence her mention to her being a "Filipina" in her very first message! Can you imagine what would happen if I went "wanna talk to a [race here] guy?", and how strange that would be?!

Message proposal 82 – 29, General Santos, Philippines
"hello 👋 ! its nice to meet you"

What can I even say about a profile in which the only textual line goes "i don't know what to say just ask"? In spite of her seven photos, this is the typical woman who wants a man to do all the effort for her!

Message proposal 83 – 40, Istanbul, Turkey
"Hi 🙂 "

Eight photos, but at least her profile says some very general lines about who she is, ranging from "Visual arts teacher and media communication teacher" to "I like to go Theater-Museum-Exhibition- Cinema" and "Vegan". I may have texted her back, if she had at least put any kind of real effort in her initial message.

Message proposal 84 – 35, Quezon City, Philippines
"So do you actually wear glasses or just for the photo?"

Ten photos, but her profile, in spite of filling every section, doesn't really talk about her, instead presenting five hearts followed by something she likes, e.g. "♡coffee". It is baffling that she fills so many sections and yet reveals so little about her. Maybe it is a sort of trick, given the way in which she tried to interact with me, which is both a fair question and one that says little about me? I'm not entirely sure.

Message proposal 85 – 40, Bangkok, Thailand
"Hi"

Six photos, five of them in sporty environments, while the last one showed her child's arm in the back of her car, as if further hinting at the fact she is a single mother. Her profile also reveals that she "love sports", but that's pretty much it.

Message proposal 86 – 28, Cebu City, Philippines
"Hii there!! Hoe are you? Hope all is well.. :) so why not give me a try? 🤭 just kidding!b hope yo talk to you soon! Keep safe"

Four photos. This one profile felt really strange to me. Like in her initial message, she repeatedly switches between a supposed truth and what seems to be her vague attempts at jokes, e.g. "Not your typical Filipina woman. Beware coz I'm crazy in a unique way! Lol. 😈 💥". I'd be wary of it, just in case, and definitely wouldn't write her back.

Message proposal 87 – 30, Jakarta, Indonesia
"Hi"

A single photo of her, with a huge smile. Her profile contains just the text "Simple life, down to earth person", along with her *Instagram* username (49 publications, 559 followers, following 395). Even if her smile was the best one in the whole world, why would I write back to someone who just wants to redirect people to her other social media?!

Message proposal 88 – 24, Moi, Kenya
"Hey [my name here], you look good"

Six photos, but all you need to know about this profile can be summed up with a phrase she wrote there - "I'm into extroverts and financially stable men with good sense of humor". Meaning, she is likely a gold-digger, and deserves to be ignored as such.

Message proposal 89 – 36, Muntinlupa, Philippines

"Hi [my name here]"

Six photos of her, including one in which she appears to be very angry at the person behind the camera. All she tells readers about her are very broad elements, such as "I enjoy life and consider myself to be outgoing bubbly and funny sometimes" and "I am carefree when i'm with genuine people". But, in this case, that one horrible picture really scared me away, since it seemed like the kind of thing you'd see from a psychopath a few minutes before getting murdered by them. I would absolutely not talk to her, at all!

Message proposal 90 – 27, Kupang, Indonesia

"Hi"

Another profile with eight photos, including a few blurry ones. Her profile only says "Hello my name is [her name here], you can call me [her nickname here]", which undoubtedly shows she puts so little effort in it as she does in everything else in her life. And why even talk to someone like that?

Message proposal 91 – 45, Rio de Janeiro, Brazil

"Hi! I am a researcher too!"

Five photos. She clearly read my profile, but describes

herself as "I am from Brazil and live in Rio de Janeiro", which is also stated in her basic profile information. Why bother writing her back if she says literally nothing about her, beside the "we're both researchers" she sent me in her first message?!

Message proposal 92 – 30, Iligan, Philippines
"hi"

Imagine you do decide to give this woman a shot, based on one of her two photos. Her profile only tells you a single thing about her, "Got no pets". This is not even worthy of sending her any kind of answer back.

Message proposal 93 – 30, Tagum, Philippines
"Hi there."

Two photos. A very similar case as the previous one, all she tells us about her is "Like to meet new faces." Why bother answering her back?!

Message proposal 94 – 30, Thôn Phong Bắc, Vietnam
"Hiiiiii Great seeing you Can I date with you?"

She did seem sweet in her six photos, but her profile literally reads "I have been single for a long time and now I want to find a boyfriend so I can comfortably hug him kiss him and cook delicious food for him share his fatigue at work, simple things for me but i still haven't found". Meaning, this is an unemployed woman who wants a boyfriend, and will literally take any single man for that, regardless of who you are. Which can be a good or a bad thing, given the fact there are many desperate men out there... hopefully, you are not one of them.

Message proposal 95 – 41, Marburg, Germany
"Hi...greeting from Bali ☺ lets do research together then ☺"

As one already seen before, this profile literally begins by correcting her location, but at least she gives us an explanation, although a bit of a strange one – "I live in Bali actually, a paradise island with full of beautiful culture. I set my place in Europe because I wanna build my relationship on it which I feel more compatible with." Besides this piece of information, each section of her profile contains just a very fickle piece of information, such as "I cook my meal everyday." But, even if I had decided to write her back, based on her six photos (four of which wearing a Covid mask), what would we even research about, since she knows nothing about mine, nor I about hers? It really sounded like a "let's say whatever and see if he writes me back at all"...

Message proposal 96 – 32, Manilla, Philippines
"The dog is photogenic :D"

A profile with five photos, in which the user does describe, through her sections, real information about her, ranging from a more basic "I enjoy reading, baking and a walk on a beach, i love food, listening to music, being with friends and family" to her goal of wanting to learn a new language. Maybe I would write her back, given her attempt to interact with my profile, even if some sections of her own are a bit basic on the information she provides.

Message proposal 97 – 31, Cebu City, Philippines
"Hi [my name here]. There's nothing wrong about trying. We never know if we won't try it. I'm [her name here] from the beautiful country of the Philippines. How you doin'?"

She said it best in her initial message, "there's nothing wrong about trying". However, she features a single photo in her profile, one where she looks at her cell phone during lunch in a restaurant, absolutely uninterested at the camera. She does provide some basic information on herself, along with her *Instagram* username (65 publications, 238 followers, following 240), but the whole thing is just incredibly bland. Even if I was to message her, and eventually meet her, what is the whole purpose of even attempting to talk to someone who, from the get-go, pretty much reveals that you're just another one of her tries, as if you were a random fish and she was somehow trying to hook you?

Message proposal 98 – 36, Montevideo, Uruguay

"Hola! Mi nombre es [her name here] 😊 We are a bit far, but it is not difficult to stop by and say "hi". You don't always come across someone cute, intelligent and committed to social causes."

Eight photos. She is going for the basic compliments, and so far so good, but the profile turns weird when she says "I look younger but I'm 43". Strangely, like her initial message, her profile is crowded with expressions in her native Spanish and English, and the translation doesn't always match up. She doesn't really say much about herself, either, apart from revealing she joined online dating following the pandemic.

Message proposal 99 – 43, Manila, Philippines
"Hi"

She does have some basic information in her profile, along with seven photos, but her notable lack of interest in her initial message would certainly make me wonder why I try to talk to her. Plus, it always seems weird when people you don't even know try to teach you how better than you they really are, i.e. "Conversation is everything, sometimes it's all you need to pull you out of the darkness, someone who's willing to listen, someone who's willing to stay, no matter how late it gets. Deep people with deep hearts and deep thoughts can sometimes save your life. They can sometimes save you from yourself."

Message proposal 100 – 36, Kennedy Town, Hong Kong
"Heyy Mate"

Likely one of the strangest profiles I have ever seen in my life. She had ten photos, but each of them were split into smaller squares, at one point diving a photo in a way that you're presented with around nine individual photos at once. There's so much going on here that I couldn't even find out what to focus in, a problem that only becomes much worse if you take into account her text features 1200 words and is completely filled with hundreds and hundreds of emojis all across, making it absurdly hard to even attempt to read any of it. As a mere example, pay a look to this section of her page:

"BTW, I'm not a Transgender, 🙅🙅🙅 Do I look like one?? 😵😵😵 In my entire existence on this planet Earth, only one doubted my IdEnTiTy. 🥴🥴🥴 Transgender are beautiful.. Am I that pretty??or Manly?? 🤪🤪🤪 Oh My Goodness.. 😅😅😅"

I definitely wouldn't write her back at all, but this profile caught my eye, just not in a very positive way. Instead, perhaps in the sense of realizing what happens when people try to go way over the top and present readers with infinitely more content than they expected. Cumulatively, when she contacted another test profile, she even repeated the exact same introductory message presented above.

By now, I had noticed I was getting way too many messages from the Philippines. According to a friend, this would be like playing online dating in easy mode, i.e. "those women just want to leave their country to have a better life, of course they're going to try to grab just any foreign man they can". As such, I stopped tracking the content of new messages from that country in the information below, but their total number of messages ended up being 84.

Message proposal 101 – 50, Edinburgh, United Kingdom

"Hello"

Seven photos. This profile literally begins with the lines "I do not live in the UK or US. And nope never been married." She then goes on to present multiple paintings and tell us more about her, but this initial line, at least for me, ruined the entire profile. Where is she is from? Where is she even located? I do not know, since she drops that bomb in the very first line but then never elaborates further on it. If nothing else, I felt this was some kind of strange scam patiently waiting to be perpetrated on me.

Message proposal 102 – 39, Budapest, Hungary

"Cute"

A cheap compliment to one of my photos is always a lousy beginning, but this profile also does not say anything about herself besides the fact she is a "Dreamer" and "Here to connect with new people". In spite of her five photos, this is way too simple and uninteresting to deserve a reply.

Message proposal 103 – 30, Yogyakarta, Indonesia

"Hey [my name here] :) . I read your profil that you're a PhD researcher. It draw my attention. I'm also researcher"

Four photos of her by the sea. Regarding herself, she only tells readers "Love adventures and doing new experiences in life. I'm pretty laid back person, understanding person, and open-minded person". If she is indeed a college researcher, as she suggested, I think that would be a much more interesting thing to add to her profile.

Message proposal 104 – 40, Bangkok, Thailand

"Nice to meet you, Mr. Gentleman ☺"

Six photos. When it comes down to sending the exact same message to every single person, this one seems to become even absurd, even more if we take into account that she says nothing significant about herself in her profile text. Why bother?

Message proposal 105 – 46, Ko Phangan, Thailand

"Hi"

A profile with 1000 words, apart from what are clearly 10 professional photos. As I read across it, it seemed to turn weirder and weirder at every corner, beginning with "NON VACCINATED GUYS ONLY!!!" (why?!), and proceeding with completely random statements such as "Was in California 9 years", "WHEN I DANCE FOR YOU MY BELOVED, I PROMISE TO SET EVERY CELL OF YOUR BEING ON FIRE !", "Children bring out the bessssssssst in me", "I also studied 'Expressive Arts therapy' in San Francisco...", "I've been through many dark nights of the soul", "NO CABLE IN MY HOME most of my 8 yrs in US, and like it that way, I do watch certain selected shows and movies on Netflix though" , "[I can't live without] Love,LOVE,loVe, lOvE, love,LoVvvvvvvvvvve". This was just too weird, I would certainly stay away from it as much as possible.

Message proposal 106 – 45, Surabaya, Indonesia

"Maybe we can get to know better"

Two photos of her, in one of which you can't even really see her face. Her profile was written in Indonesian and only featured three sentences.

Message proposal 107 – 48, Nashville, Tennessee, US

"Hi"

A single mother with a single photo in her profile, where she doesn't even show her face at all. Then, she describes herself like this - "Hopeless romantic. Loves red wine and music. Career oriented. Loves to travel. Honest. Grounded person. Living life to the fullest." - which is essentially just a bunch of general words. Skip it, evidently.

Message proposal 108 – 34, Glasston, North Dakota, US

"hi [my name here]"

A single photo, and the words "I'm just a simple girl with a big heart ❤". I wouldn't even know what to attempt to talk to her about.

Message proposal 109 – 43, Nong Song Hong, Thailand

"Woww 🙀🙀😍😍😍"

I took her emojis to mean that she somehow liked my

profile, but among her ten photos and her main point of focus being the fact she is divorced but the kid doesn't live with her, I think it is a good idea not to write back to this person. Well, at least unless you're an emoji addict.

Message proposal 110 – 40, Bucaramanga, Colombia

"Hey any plans for the holidays?"

Certainly an attractive woman, based on her eight photos, who essentially describes herself like this – "I like to see new places, try to travel often. I'm very easy going. I like to try different food. I am learning everything about meditation, law of attraction, energy etc. I love to watch funny series". There's nothing wrong with it, if it wasn't for the fact she is seemingly inviting me to something when she doesn't even know me at all.

Message proposal 111 – 41, Kuala Lumpur, Malaysia

"Hi [my name here], haha I was in the same situation. My Girlfriend signed me in without telling me 😂. We may have a few common views and interests so I got curious 😊 I love travelling, music, concerts, movies, photography, fuzzion cooking, dinner parties at home, creative table setting, Spa and all sort of relaxation. I love nature, being ECO friendly, the walk abouts, hiking and romantic snuggles, cuddles and sleepy weepies😂. And I also love dancing. It makes me feel good and sexy 😊"

Two copies of the same photo. Huge initial message, as you can certainly realize, which clearly contrasts with the fact her profile says nothing about herself. If, instead, she had bothered describing herself in her own page, she wouldn't have to send such huge messages later on...

Message proposal 112 – 32, Djibouti, Djibouti
"Hello how are you doing"

Four photos in what seems to be a beautiful traditional dress, and yet she describes herself merely as "beautiful kind". Does this mean she is both those adjectives, that she is a beautiful type of person, or something else? I could not understand, but likely she should tell people more about herself.

Message proposal 113 – 38, Toronto, Ontario, Canada
"😊 hi"

A bit of an extensive profile, but when you finally start reading it, it all crumbles into dust. It starts with "I'm on virtual travel I'm changing my location from time to time, just so you know", and presenting only two photos of herself (one of them horribly photoshopped), she then goes on to say "Not here for games, For scammers and posers get lost ...Is there any real people in here? If you ask me for photos, I would most likely ask you for a videocall, so I know I'm not being cat fished". Ah, how I love the double standards...

Message proposal 114 – 26, Johannesburg, South Africa

"Hi"

Five photos, and yet only bothers telling people that she is "A beautiful nerd. Fun, energetic and loves to travel.", which is certainly not much. Clearly, she is betting on her looks to get people to answer her.

Message proposal 115 – 52, Lisbon, Portugal

"Olá!" [i.e. "Hello!"]

Six photos and about 1000 words could usually indicate a fairly good profile, but what is a potential reader supposed to do with just the one word she decided to give me in her initial message?

Message proposal 116 – 36, San José, Costa Rica

"Simplesmente divino" [i.e. "Simply divine", presented to one of my photos]

I assume she referred to the great smile featured in one of my false photos. Her limited profile information was in Spanish – "Me encanta descubrir cosas nuevas, amo bailar, cocinar, divertirme. Desarrollar proyectos comunitarios también es lo mio" – perhaps indicating she does not speak English at all. And, if so, in spite of her four photos, how would we even be able to talk effectively? I always felt this is a significant issue that most people tend to ignore in online relationships, i.e. if you and the other person do not share a common language, you can't really interact at all, and any potential relationship will be going down the drain very, very quickly.

Message proposal 117 – 41, Medan, Indonesia

"Hi"

She only had one photo, and other than that her profile was completely empty. Why anyone would answer her message is a huge mystery to me.

Message proposal 118 – 32, Salvador, Brazil

"Oi [my name here]" [i.e. "Hi"]

Her profile only had three photos and just featured the text "Olá..." (i.e. "Hello..."). Naturally, trying to talk to her would be a complete waste of my time.

Message proposal 119 – 39, Contagem, Brazil

"Oiê!"

She says nothing about herself in her own, but chances are that she is very used up to being approached by men – out of her eight photos, six of them feature massive cleavage, and she undoubtedly has huge breasts. Unfortunately for her, that's not really what I was looking for.

Message proposal 120 – 42, Memphis, Tennessee, US

"You have beautiful eyes"

Single parent with some information in her profile. Regrettably, she also only had one photo, where she barely showed her face but actually displays massive cleavage. Not what I was looking for, really.

Message proposal 121 – 43, Bangkok, Thailand
"😍"

Six photos, a profile with barely any information about
herself, and yet she starts it by writing "They say don't
Judge a book by its cover. But if you've never noticed the
cover How do you know what's inside the book? Do you
want to open the book? Just message me", which is
essentially a silly trick not to say anything about herself.
She does, however, provide her *Instagram* username, where
she has 375 publications, 108 followers, and is following
401. Instead of all that, maybe she should have considered
telling people anything about herself.

Message proposal 122 – 30, Nairobi, Kenya
"Hey [my name here]"

Two photos. This person starts her profile with "Am not good
at explaining myself but if you get to know me you won't
regret at all" and then proceeds by never telling anything
about her at all. This is, in my view, the complete opposite
of talking about yourself – not only do you not do so, but
you somehow assure people that you're all that is great and
nothing that is bad. *Amazing*, because it also shows how
interested she is in meeting other people. One definitely has

to wonder what would happen if everyone in the world also chose to define themselves in this same way.

Message proposal 123 – 49, Pretoria, South Africa

"Hola! Uno momento, por favour. Why do you need to find a date on this site? You have the bone structure, artists want to draw, sketch and paint!☺I'm [insert name here]. Love to chat."

Eight photos, plus a profile which, here and there, revealed significant information on who she is. So far so good, but then, as I read through what she had written, some aspects of this profile made me a bit uncomfortable, such as this rant, the very first thing she displays to potential readers – "I do not play the bachelorette. If I like you, I don't keep the backdoor open! I'll give you all my attention and thus wants a man who wants me and only me as his life partner. I am not here to discuss intimacy with you or send you nude pictures of my privates. I have way to much self-respect and integrity. (intimacy talks are between lovers and not between me and you when you want online sex!!!!!!!!!!!!!) My value as a woman an person is not determined by my prowes in bed!!" And why was she even attempting to speak to me in Spanish in the first place? It truly seemed like a strange individual, regardless of her age, and I'd feel wary of answering her back, even more when she placed such an enormous emphasis on my supposed look, and that alone.

Message proposal 124 – 36, Nairobi, Kenya
"✋"

Four photos where you can barely even see her face, and her profile was filled with information which says very little to nothing about who herself - "Am proud of men who value and respect women .. .", "I get impressed with what is surrounding . which is real", "When i reach my goals what i have been dreaming of am a day dreamer.A visionary woman." What these bits of text made clear, though, is that she barely speaks English, which even further explains why her initial message to me was just an emoji.

Message proposal 125 – 38, Brooklyn, New York, US
"Hi there [my name here], I'm [her name here] nice to meet you."

She had six photos taken around the world, and her profile was actually quite well filled with information about who she is, as a person, from her background up to her current wishes and needs. Based on that, I would likely have answered her back, if it wasn't for the fact that her initial message was completely bland and far from attracting.

Message proposal 126 – 39, Montijo, Portugal
"😍"

A single photo, her profile features exclusively the text "no ONS", and her initial message is completely low-effort. For all those reasons, I don't even understand why would anyone waste their time talking to her.

Message proposal 127 – 41, São Paulo, Brazil
"Olá [my name here]" [i.e. "Hello ..."]

Nine photos, with nothing specially noteworthy about them, and a profile that, apart from featuring the photo of a puppy, didn't really say anything about her. As it is fairly common in these cases, she mentions her *Instagram* username, where she has 148 publications, 211 followers and is following 375. I wasn't even considering contacting her back, and the fact she goes for a low blow with the puppy photo – not even her own, just a generic photo taken from the web – only makes it even worse.

Message proposal 128 – 41, Jakarta, Indonesia
"Oooh my God are you a Model 😍"

Two photos, in none of which you can even clearly see her face. Then, the profile simply stated "I am funny person ☺ love do something new and love adventure😎". Given the kind of information provided, I'm not even sure why would anyone be interested in talking to her, even less given the fact she approached me exclusively based on my supposed looks, and yet failed to share her own.

Message proposal 129 – 32, Zagreb, Croatia
"Hellou Helooou.."

Six photos in her profile, in only one of which you can see her face. If you are then wondering on who she is as a person, the information "I love summer sunny days see and dolphines" is all you ever get. And, at least for me, that's clearly insufficient.

Message proposal 130 – 44, Woodbridge, Virgina, US
"Hello"

Four photos, three of them being selfies. Although she provides a four-line listing of adjectives, supposedly of her personal characteristics, the whole context makes her seem too self-centred, and her low-effort in the very first message even further confirms that idea.

Message proposal 131 – 18, Los Angeles, California, US

"You're an Author too? That's nice☺♡"

This person looked completely different in each of the four photos they had in their profile. Then, if that still wasn't fishy enough, her profile literally says this – "I'm bi and Like Daddies😝. yeah I don't like dirty Talks or sending dirty pics, so don't talk to me if that's your kink😷 and also I have a thing for men with deep voices😳😹 And I don't know if it's just the hormones talking but I think I want a Boyfriend 😝". It all seems to indicate this is a very sketchy person, and certainly one best avoided.

Message proposal 132 – 29, Bandung, Indonesia

"Hy [my name here]"

Two photos in her profile, and you can barely see her face in any of them. The profile contained three lines of very general information about her, to which she later adds that she is trying to finish an "illustrator book". A drawing, seemingly from her future book, did seem intriguing, and perhaps she should tell readers more about it. As it is, the profile is kind of incomplete, and only mere hints that it can hide, behind it, a much more interesting person than the one she very briefly alluded to. She later seems to have removed one of her photos, but contacted another test profile with the exact same initial message.

Message proposal 133 – 37, Hua Hin, Thailand
"Hi"

Three photos, along with pretty much no information on who she is, as a person – the typical indicatives of someone who is doing zero effort on any of this.

Message proposal 134 – 39, Bali, Indonesia
"Hello"

Four photos where you can barely see her, alongside with a completely empty profile. This kind of situation always intrigues me, since I just cannot understand who would ever contact such a profile, unless she was super attractive and a man was simply going for her looks.

Message proposal 135 – 31, Albuquerque, New Mexico, US
"Haha.. We're actually the same. It's just my friend who insisted me to try the app😂"

Seven photos, but something seemed very fishy to me about this profile. Among its few lines, she says "Would be nice to have a good and genuine connection with someone who is okay with meeting someone from the other side of the globe. 🌍😍". She never states where she is really from, but her look and the fact she speaks Tagalog proves that, in reality, she is actually in the Philippines, and currently misrepresenting her real location.

Message proposal 136 – 34, Santo Domingo, Dominican Republic

"Hi :)"

Ten photos, and although initially she speaks a bit about herself via a listing of adjectives, almost every area of her profile features a single short phrase, barely informative. Which is, in this case, kind of a pity, since one of her photos seems to be in a Japanese temple, and yet she barely tells people anything about such experiences. That made her seem like somewhat of a low effort profile.

Message proposal 137 – 34, Lisbon, Portugal

"Hi"

One more low-effort profile, someone misrepresenting their location, "I am a traveler and I'm traveling through Europe right now. I will be spending the new year's in Amsterdam. I'm Brazilian, I love to travel and I a work remotely. I'd like to meet new friends and who knows, something else. My job allows me to travel, so distance is not a problem. And I love europeans guys." Although she has 10 photos, among the limited information provided she states she wants "financial stability" (aka. She's a gold digger) and values "family and health".

Message proposal 138 – 29, Açu, Brazil

"Hi [first two letters of my name here]"

Six photos, including one which was just a meme putting down men. This idea, that men are bad and evil, is maintained all throughout her profile, and the reasons soon become clear - "I'm a single mom and I love kids!!! So if you don't like kids and you're only here for your own benefit, no way with me!!", i.e. she was likely made pregnant by a guy who then abandoned her. At the same time, her profile was filled with expressions in broken English, at one point stating "I'm *arretada*", a native expression that Google Translate cannot turn into English. For me, I really felt it wouldn't be a very good idea to get in touch with her, even more given her very notable anti-men stand.

Message proposal 139 – 48, Brooklyn, New York, US

"Hello [my name here]! Let's get to know each other! You sound so sweet and amazing!"

One definitely has to wonder where she got I'm "so sweet and amazing" from, since my profile was barely filled. Anyway, seven photos, with a total of 1100 words in her profile, although ordered in a bit of a non-horizontal way, with each section apparently seeming a bit different from the one that precedes it, e.g. random empty lines in the first one, bigger paragraphs in the second, bullet points in the third, a single line in the fourth, massive listings of information on the fifth, etc. Disregarding this strange inconsistency, I did end up writing her, most of all to find out why she considered me "so sweet and amazing".

Message proposal 140 – 27, Der es Salaam, Tanzania

"Hi"

Five photos in her profile, but it is very easy to recognise it as a low-effort profile when the very first sentence in her profile is "Hi, Im not good at exaplain my self.. im very open you can ask me anything...", then followed by "im looking for something serious ☺ relationship that will leads to marriage"

140

and then evidently never telling the reader anything significative about her. Just skip it already, as always in profiles similar to these.

Message proposal 141 – 34, Heredia, Costa Rica
"Hey"

Six photos, five of them being selfies and a full-body one in front of a mirror. Then, when it was time for her to talk about herself, things get weird – "I want someone who knows what he wants, I don't want anything halfway. either it is or it isn't. I don't want to waste time Or that you waste your time.. I don't like to play with anyone. I like sincerity. I am one of those who if I am interested in someone I say so, if I don't like something too. I think we are adults to be making excuses. I am affectionate, attentive, sincere. But if don't know what you want better don't waste time talking to me." With the exception of mentioning three adjectives about herself, she basically just expresses the same idea again and again, as if it was the biggest deal in the world for her. You're expecting to get to know her, and instead get this large rant which has little to do with any of it (unless it is to give you the idea that her exs did not really know what they wanted).

Message proposal 142 – 33, Utrecht, Netherlands

""

Ten photos, and then some very limited personal information, but the most noteworthy part of the profile says "I am an ordinary girl from Indonesia very simple and spontaneous person", soon followed by "♀Jakarta based *sorry to put the location randomly". It is funny that these kind of profiles, when selecting a supposedly *random* location, always find one in Europe or North America... and in this one case, she doesn't even bother attempting to explain why.

Message proposal 143 – 42, Wasior, Indonesia
"Hi [my name here] nice to see you here"

Also ten photos, then followed by a very brief "add me on What'sapp or telegram". Thank you but I'd rather not, even more since the person doesn't even say anything else about herself.

Message proposal 144 – 24, Nairobi, Kenya
"Hey"

Two photos, with the entire text on her profile then adding "someone with a big heart kind and loving..I'm an out going person..I love nature..I'm passionate about traveling and making new friends". This lack of effort she put on writing her profile is only further evidenced by her initial message to me.

Message proposal 145 – 36, Guatemala, Guatemala

"Olá! I'm glad you did!"

This one profile specially intrigued me, because, out of her 10 photos, one of them presented her winning some sort of goalkeeping award. Other than that, it was a very basic one – she just presents herself as "Funny, outgoing, sporty, loyal, down to earth and honest" – and even her initial message was lacklustre, with an initial "hello" in Portuguese followed by seemingly stating she was glad I had joined the place. I ended up messaging her, mostly over the goalkeeping photo, but this whole idea also raised a good point – maybe it'd be possible to garner some people's interest with truly intriguing photos, as I myself felt in this one case, but you'd have to focus on specific groups that may understand the real meaning behind the photo, i.e. this one case wouldn't work for a person who doesn't know what a goalkeeper is...

Message proposal 146 – 29, Jamhuri Park, Kenya

"Hi there"

Two selfies, along with the simplistic information "Outgoing, selfless, fierce woman with a big heart ♥". The classical zero-effort profile.

Message proposal 147 – 35, Buenos Aires, Argentina

" "

One more low-effort profile. Three selfies, and a small attempt at a joke – "You already have me you have 2 wishes left 😁" – but absolutely no information about her.

Message proposal 148 – 35, Jakarta, Indonesia

"Hi researcher 😊"

Six photos in random places, and three general lines about herself, the most descriptive of which went "I am kinda introvert but love to talk and make new friends." Although she read my profile, I felt hers was just too general and contradictory, and the way she referred to me seemed kind of strange, even taking into account what my own profile said.

Message proposal 149 – 39, London, United Kingdom

144

""

What can one say about a profile that literally begins with the words "I live in Colombia! I'd like to travel to London someday but I don't have plans yet!"? She had four photos, but apart from that, her profile said absolutely nothing significative about her.

Message proposal 150 – 32, Fort Mitchell, Virginia, US

"Are you a real person? Haha you seem like some simulation crafted to lure women in? 🫠. Seem to care to learn what someone is about, intelligent, cultured, care outside of your own existence and bone structure chiselled by the gods. What's the catch??"

Five photos. She did have two long paragraphs telling people about who she is as a person and what she is currently seeking, which would usually be a plus, but the name presented in her profile was literally "I'm a creeeep", which, together with the content of her initial message (what would be next? "Prove to me that you're really you"?), made it sound like she may not be exactly mentally sane. Perhaps it was all a joke, or perhaps none of these things would be necessarily bad by themselves, but when you consider the entire context at hand, I think other people would also feel wary of her.

Message proposal 151 – 31, Jakarta, Indonesia
"Hello"

One photo (with a bird at some sort of exhibition), plus a single word in her entire profile, "Hello". One certainly has to wonder how much more low-effort people can get.

Message proposal 152 – 35, Bali, Indonesia
"hello"

Ten photos, with the large majority of them seemingly having been taken in a professional studio. But then, you start reading her profile and she repeatedly says a "bad" thing, followed by somewhat of a hint that it may be a joke, i.e. "i can speak English but not really but i can uppss😹😊 and the point is i like a hairy guy too😹oh nooo but that's true😂😹". One may get really confused when it comes down to determine what is true and what isn't, even more if you consider that at one point she goes "My real name is [a name here] and [her profile name] my baptism name", which gets things even more confusing. And, regarding herself, she only says ",I'am a best girl ,loyal, honest,i like eating ,love cooking ,music". I can only imagine that

146

attempting to talk to her would require people to constantly try to figure out the difference between fact and fiction, which is not a very fun thing to have to do long-term.

Message proposal 153 – 39, Greenville, North Carolina, US

"I'm hoping to make some new friends. I teach and I'm working on my PhD in science education. What kind of research do you do?"

A single mother with eight photos, three of which doing fun stuff with her kid, and one hugging a chimp. So far so good, the whole idea seems fun, but in spite of having read my profile, hers says little about her, soon complemented with this explanatory information – "I've never done this online thing, so I'm not sure what else to say; after a long separation/ divorce process, I'm ready to um, talk to people again? Taking things slow". In this case the lack of information at least makes some sense, and for that reason I would potentially write her back, even if we are an ocean apart.

Message proposal 154 – 34, Port-of-Spain, Trinidad and Tobago

"hi handsome"

Two photos, one just of her eyes, and another displaying her massive cleavage. Then, her supposed description of herself is very basic – "I'm plus size, simple and down to earth. Ask me anything. Also msg me I can't see likes 🙈." As it is typical in other "ask me anything" profiles, this is just a very low-effort one, and deserves to be skipped.

Message proposal 155 – 23, Kampala, Uganda

"Probably your friends didn't make a mistake 👋🤭 How are you ☺"

Ten photos. For someone who writes about 220 words in her profile, there's not even a single one about herself, instead just uttering very general and idealistic sentences such as "Love is beautiful when you're heart beats for the right person no matter the distance,. Distance just gives us a reason to love HARDER". Curiously, she did have an *Instagram* username there (with 48 publications, 450 followers, following 747), but why bother talking to her when she literally never says even one word about who she is as a person?!

Message proposal 156 – 27, Pontianak, Indonesia

"Hello :)"

Six photos, with the story starting well with the information "Please read my profile first before we start a conversation. Thank you :)" From there on, it all goes down the drain, with she barely saying anything about herself, either too general (e.g. she wants to be better at cooking), or inconsequential (e.g. she loves watching Disney Princesses), to the point she even claims to want men who "have hearts for the Lord and desire to walk with Him". Given the initial line, I was definitely expecting more about her and less about topics unrelated to who she is. Oops, I guess I was completely misled – but, curiously, when she contacted another test profile, she used precisely the same opening message as here.

Message proposal 157 – 32, Pretoria, South Africa

"Hey [my name here] 🙈"

Eight photos, some of which were so heavily edited that her eyes looked like aliens'. Meanwhile, there's something very strange about starting a profile with literally the line "I have no kids and never been married." She then followed it through with a 10-bullet listing of what she enjoys (i.e. "hiking, gym, sky diving, running", and so on), ending the sequence with "I'm looking for a meaningful relationship, something that can be long term, someone who is loving, thoughtful, loyal, hard working and ambitious. No hook-ups please, Distance is not an issue." Meaning, she says more about what she wants in a guy than she ever does about who she is as a person.

Message proposal 158 – 39, Bandung, Indonesia
"hi there"

Eight photos, followed by a very brief introduction on what others say she is. That's sort of a new idea, i.e. let others attempt to describe you instead of doing it yourself, since you'll likely never get any kind of negative feedback in such a way. But that's all, two lines of text about that, and the super bland initial message.

Message proposal 159 – 39, Surabaya, Indonesia
"hai"

Seven photos, followed by a by-now typical reference to two lines of positive adjectives and the phrase "If you want to know more about me, you can message me." I'd rather not, as always in such low-effort profiles.

Message proposal 160 – 31, Min Buri, Thailand

"Narak"

Four photos, including two attempts at sexy ones in a beach. All her profile said is "Be healthy", which only gets worse when you realize that her initial message was in the language of Thailand ("narak" supposedly meaning *cute*), she seemingly doesn't even speak English, and she appeared to be currently unemployed.

Message proposal 161 – 40, Brownsville, Pennsylvania, US
"Hi"

Three selfies (where she look Philippine), along with just the text "Hi! ☺ " in her profile, is all you ever go to know about this one person. If it was possible go to under this almost bare minimum, I'm sure she would, too.

Message proposal 162 – 24, Kisumu, Kenya
"Hi"

Five photos, four of them selfies. She starts her profile by restating she is indeed from Kenya, and then proceeds with the following – "seriously looking for something serious that leads to marriage... would like to relocate outside my country as I like to try something new.. I'll be grateful to get the love of my life here from another continent" – before adding that she likes travelling. I assume she is perfect for people who want some sort of mail order bride, even more if we take into account she doesn't even say anything significant about herself, and her evident lack of effort in trying to meet someone new.

Message proposal 163 – 41, Kota Kinabalu, Malaysia

"Have a nice day"

Five photos, and she does speak a bit about herself here and there, but some of the things she wrote are strange, such as "I'm Poor in term of materials but Rich in Love. If you're looking for a rich women, you're in a wrong profile" and "Live your life with meaningful". It gets even weirder, since she mentions her *Instagram* username (26 publications, 131 followers, following 95), and her page in that other social media then forwards potential visitors to yet another different account in the same social media, making this whole thing even fishier.

Message proposal 164 – 49, Minas Gerais, Brazil

"Olá" [i.e. "Hello"]

Eight photos, one of them in a very sexy night gown, another in a very revealing wetsuit, and, unexpectedly, even one with a legendary animal from Brazil. This last photo certainly raises a million questions, but they're left completely unanswered here, even if that would be a great conversation starter. Instead, she provides three lines referencing things she likes, later complemented with a crucial piece of information – "I am not looking for anything, but open for everything! ☺" So, if she is not looking for anything at all, and from the get-go seems to make zero effort in attempting to meet anyone new, I can't even understand why would anyone contact her – and, in fact, when she contacted another test profile, she seemed equally uninterested, just uttering a mere "Ei", i.e. "Hey", in her initial message.

Message proposal 165 – 29, Jakarta Indonesia
"Hey … you dont look like 37 btw"

Ten photos, with her profile featuring almost no information, besides "I'm just a simple girl" and "Looking for a Good man who can make me smile n happy". This is very similar to the classic bare minimum effort for such content.

Message proposal 166 – 43, Bogor, Indonesia
"hi"

A single photo, where you cannot even see her face features at all, together with just the text, in Indonesian, "Hi aku orang nya mandiri, suka hal yang romatis, sayang sama keluarga" (whatever that means). Can be entirely skipped, as usual in these low-effort cases.

Message proposal 167 – 32, Copenhagen, Denmark

"cute picture"

Five photos, all of them so heavily edited with filters that they seemed more like cartoons than real photographs. This fake element is retained all through her profile, with she literally starting with the words "Switched location" and "don't match if the distance is an impediment for you... I don't want a pessimist close to me." You could, naturally, wonder where she is really from, and so her profile identifies her cumulatively as Asian, Pacific Islander, Hispanic/Latin and White, also adding that she, very unusually, speaks English, Arabic, Hebrew, Turkish and Swedish. It would be very difficult for another profile to contain as many lies as this one does in so few lines.

Message proposal 168 – 32, Denpasar, Indonesia

"Hi [my name here]"

Three photos, in none of which you can see her face well. Although her profile contained some information about who she is, none of it was significative, e.g. "Likes to cook but hate doing dishes", "saving up for euro trip", "like cats". Since she openly admitted her age was wrong, one must certainly ask how serious she is about trying to meet someone, if at all.

Message proposal 169 – 34, Jakarta, Indonesia

"Hi"

A single photo wearing a burka, meaning you could only see her eyes and forehead. All you get to hear about her is that she is "Looking for serious partner" and "if you want to know about me, let's talk." The classic low-effort profile, and one you should always skip.

Message proposal 170 – 37, Port Moresby, Papua New Guinea

"Hello I'm Tiizz from Papua New Guinea"

Three photos, one of which was just an inspirational quote by one Jose Harris. About her, you only learn that she is "Simple,kind, humble and honest", and that "swimming and diving my favourite". Naturally, this is yet another of those profiles that you can simply skip, even more since her initial message simply repeated what her profile always has to include.

Message proposal 171 – 31, Ho Chi Minh City, Vietnam

"Love your dog. Nice to chat with you"

Five photos, one of which was simply a collection of photos from some other undisclosed app. She said nothing about herself, but alluded to the fact that she was seeking her "soulmate". As usual, such a profile does not really deserve your time at all.

Message proposal 172 – 27, Nairobi, Kenya

"Title of your favorite book? One that you've written"

Six photos, and all you get to learn about her is that she is a kenyan-born woman living in Kenya and "looking for a single man who values honesty and is looking to date/ get into a relationship". Why even bother with such a profile, unless you're super desperate for having any kind of... anything with a woman?

Message proposal 173 – 39, ?

"Hello, you have 2 profiles on this app?"

An extremely fishy profile, since it repeatedly changed its location and the number of photos it has (at the lowest, two; at the highest I've seen, five), while retaining all the text in her profile, which always stated she was "here to connect with people from all over the world" but also specifically "looking for you". At the same time, her initial message is, in my view, among the most interesting I've seen – by selling the reader an idea that someone else may be copying their profile (or, more often, stealing their photos), she definitely incites significant interest from the person reading the message, who would usually answer her back hoping, at the very least, to learn more about what may be going on. Although such strategy would not work in my specific case, I openly recognise this is a very interesting technique that could certainly work for most people.

Message proposal 174 – 44, Bangkok, Thailand
"Hello"

A profile with ten photos, but only a single line about herself, i.e. "I live happily love exercise and want to meet good people". For hilarity's sake, she then follows her speech directly with the following lines, "I don't want scammers to scam.Don't waste my time trying to fool me I'm not a fool. Do not want to invest or stocks trading", which shows she cares more about referencing potential scammers than she ever does about presenting herself to potential readers. Her low-effort initial message follows through with that same idea, showing you should not waste any of your time on her.

Message proposal 175 – 36, El Cajon, California, US

"Hi [my name here], you have a great smile and your eyes are pretty."

Seven photos, in almost all of which she displayed massive cleavage. So, her interest in my own supposed good looks, evidenced in the initial message, become very easy to understand, but she doesn't tell people much about herself, instead just giving us all a very tenuous "I'm a fun person, respectful. I like to go to the beach sometimes, I like outdoors activities." So, unless I was looking for a beautiful body and nothing else, talking to her would be a huge waste of time.

Message proposal 176 – 42, Stirling Castle, Jamaica

"You sound like a kind hearted person [my name here]"

Six photos, two of them taken directly from some other undisclosed app. One definitely has to wonder where she actually got I may be "a kind hearted person" from my own super brief introduction. But, leaving aside that issue, she wrote many things in her profile, ranging from a brief introduction – "Classy lady who is happy to use a circular saw. I like creating things." – to some very oddly specific elements, such as "I hum for no apparent reason and dance sometimes even when you can't hear the music", and even completely contradictory pieces of information, e.g. "extroverted introvert", "sweet and a little sour". She later complements those with very specific references to what she is looking for – "the king to my queen...my very own romance story and all the awesome and not so awesome that comes with it but makes us stronger" and "A man looking for something serious, leading to marriage. I'm looking for my forever man. Someone who believes in God. Who isn't afraid to go for what he wants. Someone to laugh and enjoy life with. Someone to love and be loved by, in spite of our shortcomings." This, together with all the information she provides about herself, makes the entire thing sound like a complete fantasy, one that no real man will ever be able to fulfil, which may even explain why she remains single at the age of 42.

Message proposal 177 – 36, Jakarta, Indonesia
"Hello [my name here] ☺"

Seven photos, with nothing specially noteworthy in them.
She doesn't say much about herself either, apart from "I am
very affectionate, sweet, loyal, honest, oriented family, and
always smiling", but does provide her *Instagram* username,
a private profile where she has 76 publications, 463
followers, and is following 622. And, of course, she is
looking for a "serious relationship", which may be hard to
find given how little she tells us about herself and how basic
her initial message was.

Message proposal 178 – 33, Jakarta, Indonesia
"mt.fuji?"

A single photo, where you cannot even see her face, then
followed by just one phrase in her profile, i.e. "welcome to
my upside down world!!" Why anyone would even talk to
her is unknown, this is literally the minimum possible
information for a profile, even if she tried to interact with
one of my profile photos a bit.

Message proposal 179 – 39, Husavik, Iceland

"I would like to get to know you, will you give me the chance?"

Three photos, one of which with a giant cartoon pig statue, where she was clearly Asian. Although such an idea may seem quaint, when it comes to talking about herself she just tells people she is "Down to the earth.. Grateful..", and nothing else. And, although based in her initial message you could think she was specifically interested in talking to me, the rest of her profile makes it clear she is interested in getting to know just anyone at all, with no specific requirements. A complete catch for any man who wants just literally any female human being in his life, I'd say.

Message proposal 180 – 34, Cope, Angola
"Hi"

Six photos, two of them simply of local landscapes from her country. And then, when it comes to talking about herself, she simply says "God will meet you where you are in order to take you where he wants you to go", followed by three proverbs in Portuguese. Once more, I have no real idea why anyone would interact with this profile, perhaps unless they are seeking a tourist guide in Angola.

Message proposal 181 – 38, Nairobi, Kenya

"Hi"

Four photos, three of them being horrendous selfies, then
followed by a single line in her profile, "am Lucy God fearing
woman,am a business lady". For some reason, the "god-
fearing" line appears to be common in Kenya, but it is clear
this one is not very interested in getting to know anyone,
given her notable low-effort in all of this.

Message proposal 182 – 40, Lisbon, Portugal
"Hi [my name here]! How have you been? We live very
close, I guess☺"

Six photos, two of them being selfies, along with one at a
gym. Her profile merely displayed a small poem, "Little by
little/ Day by day/ What is meant to be/ Will always find a
way ☺", which would be unusual in a positive way, if it
wasn't for the fact that she doesn't tell us anything about
who she is. The fact she seemingly approached me based
on our location being close matters little if we consider I
know nothing about her and, as such, have no sufficient
reasons to write her back.

Message proposal 183 – 40, Zurich, Switzerland
"Hi👋👋I'm [her real(?) name here] nice to meet you"

Seven photos, all of them taken in Thailand, and so a reader has no reason to believe she is really in Switzerland – and yet, nothing in her profile alludes to this incorrect location, or for a potential reason behind it. Instead, she says "If you want to get to know me better, match me and chat with me", which is, as you'll certainly know by now, the very indicative of a low-effort profile. She later contacted another test profile with a very similar message, simply adding two emojis to the end.

Message proposal 184 – 42, Jakarta, Indonesia
"Hey.... I can see your eyes 👀"

Ten photos, but a profile mostly written in Indonesian. I could not read the language at all, and as such I'd have little reason to talk to her.

ANNEX 2 – Age of the people who contacted me

Age	
18-20	2
21-30	49
31-40	97
41-50	35
51-60	1
61-70	0
71-80	0
81-90	0

ANNEX 3 – Reported location of people who contacted me

Location	
Unknown	1
Angola	1
Argentina	1
Brazil	10
Bulgaria	1
Canada	2
China	1
Colombia	1
Costa Rica	4
Croatia	1
Denmark	1
Djibouti	1
Dominican Republic	2
Germany	3
Guatemala	1
Hong Kong	1
Hungary	1
Iceland	1
Indonesia	43

Jamaica	1
Kenya	9
Malaysia	2
Mexico	3
Netherlands	1
Panama	1
Papua New Guinea	2
Philippines	38 (+ 46)[15]
Poland	1
Portugal	5
Romania	1
Singapore	1
South Africa	3
Switzerland	1
Tanzania	2
Thailand	12
Trinidad and Tobago	1
Turkey	2
Uganda	1
UK	2
Uruguay	1
US	14

---

15 As explained among the data I collected, after 100 entries I stopped
    compiling data from the Philippines, but still registered their number of
    new messages here, between parenthesis.

Vietnam	2
Zambia	1

ANNEX 4 – Number of words in initial messages

Number of words	
0^{16}	9
1	65
2	28
3	7
4	8
5	8
6	12
7	11
8	3
9	4
10	4
11	1
12	2
13	0
14	4
15	0
16	1
17	2

16 This number could only be achieved if they sent me a message with just emojis. I did not count emojis as words.

18	1
19	2
20	0
21	1
25	1
27	1
28	1
32	1
33	1
34	1
35	1
44	3
84	1

ANNEX 5 – Number of photos in each profile

Number of photos	
1	17
2	13
3	18
4	21
5	16
6	35
7	13
8	13
9	7
10	31

ANNEX 6 – Would I message them?

Would I message them?	
Yes	11
No	173

ANNEX 7 – Messages from *Bumble* Customer Support

In late 2022 I tried to create an account on an online dating app named *Bumble*. As I was going through the very first steps of the process, literally *all* photos I attempted to submit were censored by their staff – and I initially attempted all their submissions twice! They were all completely harmless[17], and so I started by reading their photo rules – which I then pointed out I had read – and subsequently contacted their Customer Support, trying to find an explanation for this absurd censorship. What follows are copies of their subsequent answers to this simple question, i.e. "I submitted multiple photos to you, why were they all censored?", when I tried to get an answer to what would essentially seem like a very simple question.

Hello,
Thanks for getting in touch.
I've looked into this and can see your photo was moderated as it contained text (including emojis or

---

17 For information on their precise content, check "Chapter 2".

stickers), or it wasn't an original photo. A few other guidelines are listed here also: [link here].
Our records show that profiles with clear, original photos receive more matches, and we're sure this is exactly what you want!
Please let me know if I can help with anything else.
Chloe
Bumble Feedback Team

I had submitted multiple photos, not just one (as the message reports), and so I replied them back with the exact same issue as before. This time, I got this answer:

Hello,
Thanks for getting back to us.
I can see your photo was removed because it contains text or a watermark. Please also know that we cannot accept photos that have been heavily edited.
Our records show that profiles with clear, original photos receive more matches, and we're sure this is exactly what you want!
I apologise for any inconvenience.
Noah

Bumble Feedback Team

Again, this only referred to one photo. Meanwhile, I tried to submit them all again, this time they accepted a single one out of all six I had submitted. I kept on asking about the problem with the remaining ones, when I received this answer:

Hello,
Thanks for getting back to us.
We can see one of these photos is currently active on your profile and the other was moderated for the reasons we have already explained.
Please, let us know if there is anything else we can help you with.
Noah
Bumble Feedback Team

Yes, the "other" was supposedly "moderated for the reasons we have already explained", except that I had submitted more than two, and all the others were still being censored. I wanted to know why, and so I tried yet again. Around this time I had submitted a GDPR data request, and so they merged the two tickets to avoid answering to this whole issue. I kept on pressing for an answer, and I got this massive one, where they pasted two automated messages together and even left out the name of the replier:

Hi there [my name here],
Thank you for your mail regarding your photos got moderated.
It seems like your photo got moderated because your full face wasn't visible in the photo so for future reference you can refer to the information given below.
Bumble is the first app to bring dating, friend-finding and career-building to a single platform, being a social network rooted in promoting kindness, respect and empowerment.
To make sure everybody is aligned, our guidelines are designed to ensure every member has a safe and enjoyable experience on Bumble. We have a team of moderators working 24/7 to guarantee that all photos follow our guidelines. Below, you have a general overview of our rules for pictures:
- If a photo isn't yours and you don't have permission to use it, don't add it

- Your kids are totally cute, but they can't be on your profile picture unless you are in the photo, too
- Absolutely no nudity or pornography
- No photos of any type of illegal activity. That means no pictures of drug usage or abusive and obscene behavior
- Bikinis and swimwear pics are only okay if you are outdoors; for example, in a pool or at the beach. But if you're indoors, that's a no-no, since it looks too much like underwear
- On that note, no pictures in your underwear either. And men, no shirtless photos—unless you're at the beach
- Photos with friends are allowed, but you have to include at least one photo of yourself where you can clearly see your face. We want to know who you are!
- No photos that include guns, unless the person is a member of the military or a law enforcement officer in uniform
- Your face has to be clearly visible in every single one of the photos you upload to your profile. No hiding behind your phone or your hair, please
- No pictures with dead or dying animals where they are bloody or have a gun pointed at them

176

- No watermarks or text overlaid over photos
- Photos with no people will be removed
Bear in mind failure to adhere to these guidelines may result in losing access to our platform.
I hope I was able to help you out today.
If there is anything else we can do for you, please don't hesitate to get in touch.
We wish you meaningful connections and good matches!
Have a lovely day!
Thanks for reaching out to Bumble! It looks like we have resolved your query. If you need anything else at all, please don't hesitate to let us know. All you have to do is reply within 48 hours and we will be in touch.
Bumble Feedback Team

As you may easily notice, this refers to a single photo – the only one they'd already told me about before – and not to the fact they'd initially censored all of the ones I had submitted, and by now had only accepted a single one. So, I asked the exact same question yet again:

Hi there [my name here],

Thanks for getting in touch.

There is overlaid text visible in two of the photos shown in your screenshot which is why they were moderated. The other is currently active on your profile which means it was moderated by mistake. Please, let us know if there is anything else we can help you with.

Noah

Bumble Feedback Team

Finally, I got an answer that refers to three – out of six – photos, although only one of them had "overlaid text". They admitted that the removal of one of them was a mistake. Getting this answer "just" took five days and multiple efforts. But, still hoping to get answers on the remaining ones, I asked about it again and got this answer:

Hello,

Thanks for reaching out!

I'm sorry you've not had a positive experience on Bumble so far. We continually review feedback to improve our app, and we're grateful you took the time to share this with us.

178

Let me know if there's anything else I can help you with.
Nadja
Bumble Feedback Team

Yet again, this helped me in absolutely no way at all, even more if we take into account I had shared no direct feedback with them. I asked again, and got this answer:

Hi there [my name here],
Thanks for reaching out.
We are sorry if your question wasn't answer as timely as we aim to, we try to get back to everyone as soon as we can.
Have a lovely day!
Nadja
Bumble Feedback Team

This time, they completely ignored the problem and made it sound as if I was complaining about the time it took them to answer me back, something I never did. And yet, they kept on ignoring the fact they'd censored six of my photos, even after five days.

Next one followed:

Hello,

Thank you for your outreach.

I've taken a look over your correspondence and it appears as though my colleagues have been able to fully resolve your queries.

To ensure we are providing efficient support to our entire community, we will be closing this thread for the time being.

If you need anything in the future related to your account, please don't hesitate to get back in touch.

Thanks so much for your understanding.

Thanks for reaching out to Bumble! It looks like we have resolved your query. If you need anything else at all, please don't hesitate to let us know. All you have to do is reply within 48 hours and we will be in touch.

Nadja

Bumble Feedback Team

This time, given the very nature of their answer, I revealed that all their messages were going to be published in this book and later in a peer reviewed study about online dating. Suddenly, I seemed to

matter a lot more and the whole nature of their
answers changed completely:

Hi there [my name here],
Thank you for your recent email. We are happy to see
you are part of our Hive!
I apologise that you're not happy with the answers
you've received. Bumble takes the quality of our
customer support very seriously, and we always
appreciate feedback like yours to improve the quality
of our help.
Reading through your case, as two of your pictures
were moderated for the same reason, my colleagues
generally mentioned the main concern instead of
mentioning the reason separately. Our bad!
We do, however, consistently reinforce to our
members the importance of pictures that clearly shows
someone's face, the reason we use "Our records show
that profiles with clear, original photos receive more
matches, and we're sure this is exactly what you
want!".
Many of our members think their pictures show their
faces visibly. Still, it's not always the case, and we
have to share this message, even if it sounds not the

case from another person's perspective, as it's usually
the main reason why pictures are moderated.
Again, we're sorry for the experience; your feedback
was noted.
Thanks for using Bumble, and we hope you find
meaningful connections with us.
Esther
Bumble Feedback Team

So, long story short, I opened an account in their app, submitted six photos, they censored *all* of them, and yet never really explained me *why*. After a lot of tries, I randomly managed to get *one* of them accepted, got the admission that another *one* was removed because it had overlaid text (they mention two, but only one ever had it), and that *another* was removed "by mistake". The censorship of the remaining three photos will remain a mystery until the end of time.

ANNEX 8 – GDPR Request with *Bumble*

As mentioned in the previous annex, at one point I filed a GDPR request with *Bumble*. After waiting past the legal period to receive that data, I eventually contacted their "Data Protection Officer" and finally ended up getting a copy of my personal data. In this specific case, it included:

- A copy of all my photos they had accepted to use in their website (just one, in my particular case), along with metadata related to them, specifically a "Signature" and a "Vector", which certainly allows them to identify this photo in the future, if I ever submitted it again, either in the original format or with some significant changes.

- Billing History related to my profile, including sections labelled "Payments history", "Credits history", "Subscription history", "Payment details history", "Refunds history" and "Chargeback history".

- This profile's IP History, which is a listing of all the IP addresses I had used this account on.

- All image files I submitted to their customer support, along with *some* of the messages I had sent to them, and some they had replied back to me. Strangely, but also very conveniently, this compilation does not contain the final message reproduced in the previous annex, nor any of the messages I sent to them afterwards, in spite of having been compiled at a later date, meaning they are literally – and *illegally*! – hiding information from requesters.

- Finally, and perhaps most interesting of them all, I received a "report" explicitly labelled "released for intelligence purposes only", which contained my e-mail address, site id, name and nickname, gender, location, age, date of birth, registration and last login date. But it continued with even more information – profile language, whether I have tattoos and piercings[18], a listing of my previous profile texts, my linked social networks and phone numbers, my swipe data, my GPS

---

18 This raises a very good question – since people are never explicitly asked for this information, how did they collect it? Do they have a team verifying all photos, one by one, to compile this information? Even if they do, why do they have specific interest in these elements? That's another true mystery for the ages.

data, what specific users I reported and, finally, when did I put my profiles in snooze mode.

===== The End! =====